SITTING IN: JAZZ PIANO

Backing Tracks and Improv Lessons

NOAH BAERMAN

JEN ALLEN

In addition to the MP3 demonstrations and backing tracks, the companion DVD includes Alfred's exclusive TNT 2 software, which allows users to customize the audio tracks in this book for practice. Use it to slow down tracks, isolate and loop parts, and change tempos and keys.

To install, insert the DVD into the disc drive of your computer.

Windows

Double-click on **My Computer**, right-click on the DVD drive icon, and select **Explore**. Open the **TnT2** folder and double-click on the installer file.

Macintosh

Double-click on the DVD icon on your desktop. Open the **TnT2** folder and double-click on the installer file.

TNT 2 SYSTEM REQUIREMENTS

Windows
XP, Vista, 7, 8
QuickTime 7.6.7 or higher
1.8 GHz processor or faster
3.1 GB hard drive space
2 GB RAM minimum
DVD drive for installation
Speakers or headphones
Internet access for updates

Macintosh
OS 10.4 and higher (Intel only)
QuickTime 7.6.7 or higher
3.1 GB hard drive space
2 GB RAM minimum
DVD drive for installation
Speakers or headphones
Internet access for updates

Alfred Music
P.O. Box 10003
Van Nuys, CA 91410-0003
alfred.com

Copyright © MMXIV by Alfred Music
All rights reserved. Printed in USA.

No part of this book shall be reproduced, arranged, adapted, recorded, publicly performed, stored in a retrieval system, or transmitted by any means without written permission from the publisher. In order to comply with copyright laws, please apply for such written permission and/or license by contacting the publisher at alfred.com/permissions.

ISBN-10: 1-4706-1556-8 (Book & DVD-ROM)
ISBN-13: 978-1-4706-1556-7 (Book & DVD-ROM)

Audio recorded and mixed by Collin Tilton at Bar None Studio, Northford, CT
Kris Allen (saxophone), Rich Goldstein (guitar), Henry Lugo (bass), Ben Bilello (drums)
Piano performed by Noah Baerman and recorded by Norman Johnson at Manor Recording, Middletown, CT

Cover Photos
Guitarist: © iStockphoto / Jan Kowalski • Saxophonist: © Digital Vision • Keyboardist: Dale Berman • Bassist: © moodboard / Corbis • Drummer: © iStockphoto / Aleksandar Georgiev
Author photos: Noah Baerman © Kate Ten Eyck • Jen Allen © Ben Stamper

Alfred Cares. Contents printed on environmentally responsible paper.

CONTENTS

SONGS BY CATEGORY

In addition to the TNT 2 software (with its own set of audio tracks), MP3s are also included on the accompanying DVD-ROM. The symbol shown to the left appears next to every song in the book and is used to identify the TNT 2 tracks and MP3s on the DVD ("Track 1," "Track 2," "Track 3," etc.).

To access the MP3s on the DVD, insert the DVD into the disc drive of your computer. In Windows, double-click on My Computer, then right-click on the DVD icon labeled "Sitting In – Jazz Piano" and select Explore to view the "MP3s" folder and copy it to your hard drive. For Mac, double-click on the DVD icon on your desktop labeled "Sitting In – Jazz Piano" to view the "MP3s" folder and copy it to your hard drive.

ABOUT THE AUTHORS

Noah Baerman (www.noahjazz.com) earned bachelor's and master's degrees in jazz studies from Rutgers University in the 1990s, studying under Kenny Barron. To date, Noah has released nine jazz albums under his own name. His widely acclaimed 2003 release *Patch Kit* raised funds and awareness for Ehlers-Danlos Syndrome, a connective tissue disorder with which he was born. That album, featuring bassist Ron Carter and drummer Ben Riley, also led to an appearance for Noah on Marian McPartland's NPR program Piano Jazz. Most recently he released *Ripples*, an acclaimed and diverse album of Noah's original compositions. *Ripples* was produced in conjunction with Resonant Motion, Inc., a non-profit organization for which Noah serves as Artistic Director.

Noah is active as an educator, directing the Jazz Ensemble at Wesleyan University and teaching at numerous other institutions. He has written many instructional books for Alfred Music, including the three-volume *Complete Jazz Keyboard Method* and *The Big Book of Jazz Piano Improvisation*. He lives in Middletown, CT with his wife, visual artist Kate Ten Eyck, and has three daughters.

PHOTO BY KATE TEN EYCK

Jen Allen (www.jenallenmusic.com) received her bachelor's degree in 2000 from The Jackie McLean Institute of Jazz at the Hartt School, where she studied under McLean and other jazz luminaries including Steve Davis, Nat Reeves, Andy Laverne, and Harold Danko. Jen was one of eight pianists worldwide chosen to participate in the Mary Lou Williams Women in Jazz Workshop in 2011, a year that also saw her perform at the Kennedy Center and the release of her debut recording, *Pieces of Myself*. She regularly appears as a bandleader and sideman at major jazz venues throughout New York City and the Northeastern United States. Jen is a visiting lecturer at Trinity College, where she directs the jazz ensemble and teaches jazz history and music business. She is also on the faculty of the University of Hartford, teaching music theory and history. Since 2011, Jen has been a senior teaching artist for Litchfield Performing Arts, Inc., and is the director of their Connecticut regional jazz combo program. She lives in West Hartford, Connecticut with her husband, saxophonist Kris Allen and their two children.

PHOTO BY BEN STAMPER

ACKNOWLEDGMENTS

Jen and Noah would like to thank Nat Gunod, Burgess Speed, Timothy Phelps, Ron Manus, Link Harnsberger, and the whole Alfred Music team. Thanks to Collin Tilton at Bar None Studios for knowing just what to do to capture the sounds and Norman Johnson at Manor Recording for putting the icing on that cake. Thanks to Kris Allen, Rich Goldstein, Henry Lugo, and Ben Bilello for giving everyone using this book such a vital and swinging aural context for their studies.

Noah would like to thank Jen Allen for being a sharp, wise, and inspiring collaborator on this project. Thanks to Henry Lugo, Vinnie Sperrazza, Kris Allen, Jimmy Greene, Chris Dingman, Amanda Monaco, Wayne Escoffery, Jay Hoggard, and all the other musicians who continue to provide stimulation, inspiration, and friendship. Thanks to Kenny Barron, George Raccio, and all the other teachers (living and not) who have made me who I am. Thanks to Mo Sila, Rachel Green, Dawn Revett, Karl and Beth Mueller, Dave Kopperman, Christine Caruso, the RMI team, Marty Khan, the whole Peace Posse, and all the other friends who nourish my soul. Thank you to Rebecca, Ariana (and Tyler), and Tiana for reminding me what it's all about. And thanks to Kate for everything, all the time.

Jen would like to thank Noah for being an encouraging, knowledgeable, and amazingly talented coauthor. Thanks to Jonathan Barber, Matt Dwonszyk, Henry Lugo, Andrew Renfroe, Yunie Mojica, and Raynel Frasier for pushing me into new realms of music. Thank you to Jackie McLean, Andy LaVerne, Nat Reeves, Steve Davis, and to my many teachers over the years who have poured words of wisdom into my musical soul. Thanks to Mom, Al, Beth Clark, Jim Clark-Stewart, the whole Damiani clan, Nelba Marquez-Greene, Jimmy Greene, the Peace Posse, Hannah Jackson, Kate Hughes, Carilta Elias, Elizabeth Zagata, Susie Huang, and Renee Kleinman, for your love, prayers, understanding spirits, and words of encouragement. Thank you to Avery and Rory for always inspiring me to live and love more fully. Thanks to Kris for being my love, spiritual partner, and rock in all things.

HOW TO USE THIS BOOK

Each *etude* (study) in this book was carefully crafted using a standard progression in the jazz repertoire. We call them etudes here because they were created to help you develop your jazz vocabulary and fluency, but really they are also full-fledged jazz tunes. These chord progressions relate to songs that are essential for a fluent jazz musician to know, and they cover a wide range of the tune types and general challenges that create literacy in jazz performance.

For each song, there is a Roadmap that tells you the exact layout of the tune on the audio recording. You will also find a brief synopsis with an overview of what makes that chord progression distinctive and how it is generally approached in real-life musical situations. Additionally, you will get listening suggestions, all available through various online sources (iTunes, Amazon, Spotify, Rhapsody, etc.). This listening component is essential for absorbing the rhythmic, harmonic, and melodic devices and nuances that lead to jazz fluency and authenticity.

Each lesson that follows introduces standard ways of improvising (soloing and/or comping) over the tune's chord progression. While this is not a "method book" per se (presuming to give you a comprehensive path to fluency), the etudes and the lessons that accompany them are ordered for a steady increase in challenge.

Finally, you can refer to the appendix (starting on page 70) for useful information about scales, chords, harmony, and jazz voicings.

WORKING WITH THE DVD-ROM

The DVD-ROM features three sets of play-along options to allow for maximum versatility in your practicing. You get the following:

- An MP3 recording of each tune with a quartet of piano, saxophone, bass, and drums

- An MP3 recording of each tune with a quartet of saxophone, guitar, bass, and drums

- TNT 2 software, which provides a tremendous capacity to isolate and loop sections, choose which instruments you want in the mix, and even to change tempos and keys

In each case, you get multiple choruses of each etude, played by a top-notch professional jazz combo. Each etude contains a statement of the written melody (or "head"), followed by a saxophone solo and space for a piano solo before the head is restated. The precise length of each of these portions is laid out in the Roadmap on the page of the book with the etude itself.

The first set of MP3s (with piano) acts less as a play-along and more as a demonstration, with the piano offering some straightforward soloing and comping ideas and examples of what you can play over these tracks.

The second set of MP3s (without piano) contains the backing tracks. In these, the saxophone gives you melodic reinforcement as you play the head or allows you to comp while he plays the head. The saxophone solo provides some stylistically appropriate soloing ideas while giving you a further opportunity to comp for a soloist. The guitar helps to support and reinforce your comping, which is particularly useful if you are still developing your fluency in comping with your left hand as you solo with your right.

The TNT 2 software offers a whole host of other options. You can choose which instruments are in the mix. The transposition option allows you to try the songs out in different keys, while the tempo-changing option can help both in the early stages, where you may need to slow down the tempos of the songs, and in the more advanced stages, where you may want to add a further layer of challenge by speeding them up. The possibilities may not be literally endless, but they're pretty close!

BU'S BLUES
(Blues)

Roadmap

8 total choruses:
2 choruses of head (melody), 2 choruses of saxophone solo, 2 choruses of piano solo, 2 choruses of head out.

Art Blakey (1919–1990) was an influential drummer and the leader of the important jazz combo The Jazz Messengers. The Messengers were known for nurturing talented musicians who would later go on to important careers of their own. Through the years, the piano "chair" alone featured such all-stars as Horace Silver, Walter Davis, Jr., Bobby Timmons, Cedar Walton, Mulgrew Miller, and many others.

PHOTO COURTESY OF INSTITUTE OF JAZZ STUDIES, RUTGERS UNIVERSITY

Overview

"Bu's Blues" is a tribute to the great drummer and bandleader Art Blakey. The 12-bar blues progression is the most common in all of jazz, and the three-chord version represented by this tune is the most straightforward variant of it, heard in blues, R&B, and early rock and roll, in addition to jazz. The simplicity of the chord progression affords us a great deal of flexibility in our approach. We can play simply and melodically, making this a perfect starting point for less experienced improvisers or people looking to emote the blues with a minimum of chord-based obstacles. On the other hand, more advanced players have the option of using the simple chords as a relatively unencumbered jumping-off point for more elaborate and harmonically adventurous soloing and comping.

Listening Suggestions

Duke Ellington: "C Jam Blues"
This 1942 recording (reissued on numerous compilations like *Never No Lament: the Blanton-Webster Band*) is an elegant but hard-swinging interpretation of straightforward blues chords. Ray Nance, Rex Stewart, Ben Webster, "Tricky Sam" Nanton, and Barney Bigard all solo, as well as the Duke himself on piano. This classic song is sometimes known as "Duke's Place."

Sonny Rollins: "Blue 7"
This track from the classic 1956 *Saxophone Colossus* album features some great soloing and rhythm section work by pianist Tommy Flanagan and drummer Max Roach. Sonny himself, on tenor saxophone, gives a clinic in thematic development, as he displays his assimilation of his Thelonious Monk influence by creatively repeating and elaborating on relatively straightforward musical ideas for chorus after chorus.

Jimmy Smith: "Back at the Chicken Shack"
The title track of Jimmy Smith's 1960 album demonstrates how Smith turned the Hammond organ into a go-to instrument for soulful blues-based tunes, especially using the swinging "shuffle" rhythm heard here. Other soloists on this tune include Stanley Turrentine on tenor saxophone and Kenny Burrell on guitar, two other masters of the "soul jazz" sound.

John Coltrane: "Chasin' the Trane"
It is remarkable to think that this 16-minute tour-de-force is based on just these three chords and this simple 12-measure form. Coltrane recorded this song at New York's famed Village Vanguard in 1961 accompanied only by Reggie Workman on bass and Elvin Jones on drums, and his tenor saxophone soloing is passionate and endlessly inventive. As with his recording of "Take the Coltrane" with Duke Ellington, he shows how much a soloist can add to a simple three-chord blues.

Blues tunes offer a jumping-off place for musicians of all levels, so playing on a blues will be our foundation for improvising in this book. Harmonically and rhythmically, playing on a blues will help you with all the other chord progressions we will look at later.

Actually sounding like you are playing a blues is important. The great saxophonist and composer Jackie McLean used to emphasize this with students, re-directing those consumed with displaying their technique or their coolest licks with a simple statement of "that was good but I didn't hear the blues!" In other words, it's not how much you play, it's how you play it.

Improvising on "Bu's Blues"

Let's jump right in. For starters, when playing the blues, using a "bluesy" sound is necessary. Obvious, right? In order to achieve this sound, we use the blues scale. The notes for a blues scale are 1, ♭3, 4, ♯4, 5, ♭7. See the appendix on page 72 for more on this.

When a blues scale is used over the whole blues chord progression of I–IV–V, this is considered to be a *horizontal* way of improvising. You are using one scale to play over all the chords that are going by rather than adapting to each individual chord. A horizontal approach will also be used in many other tunes. Learning it in the context of a blues is the most basic way to understand horizontal playing.

Check out this example, which uses the horizontal approach over the first four measures.

Measures 1–4

Running up and down the blues scale, however, will not give you the desired result of sounding like you know what you are doing. How you play the blues scale is just as important as knowing the notes. To sound authentic, you want to focus on phrasing and rhythmic ideas.

Phrasing in a blues often takes the form of *call and response*. Call and response is a key element of the blues sound. The 12 bars are divided into three 4-measure phrases. The first 4 measures can be used to state a phrase. Then it can be repeated (with or without slight variations) in measures 5–8. Then the pivotal response to the call typically happens in measures 9–12. This is where you get to let loose a little bit!

Let's start with a limited amount of notes so we can focus on the rhythmic accents as well as the phrasing. Too many notes can sound like rambling. Simple can be SO good! Take three notes from the blues scale and practice simple but rhythmic phrases that repeat. Simple is also good because you will have to be able to repeat back what you play. If the phrase is too difficult, it will be hard to play again.

Here's an example over the first 4 measures.

Measures 1–4

The first thing to notice in the previous example is that the phrase doesn't start on beat 1. Starting on a beat other than 1 keeps you from being really predictable. As you start to play this phrase, it is important to recognize which notes you want to accent. In the first phrase the accent comes on the "and" of 3. This continues throughout the piece.

The notes are F#, G, and C, though the octave of the C changes in the second measure. Notice that the rhythmic placement of the phrase is altered in measure 4. This adds a little interest to the phrase. When at a loss, changing one simple thing can really enhance a musical idea.

Let's do the next four measures.

Measures 5–8

As you can see, the notes are the same in measures 5 and 6 even though the chord is different. The rhythmic idea has changed just slightly. In measure 7, the notes and rhythm are almost the same as the beginning. Again, small changes can do a lot.

The last four measures are where the answer or response comes. Note that a suggested left-hand accompaniment is included here as well.

Measures 9–12

This phrase ends up using more of the blues scale (actually the whole thing!) in a typical blues language phrase. We will explore more of what this "language" is as we move forward. In the meantime, notice the rhythm and the accents. This musical idea is totally different than the others. It is a real response to what was stated before.

As you can see, the call and response in this blues, though simple, really leaves you with a complete musical idea. Call and response is one of the most basic ideas in music. When musical ideas repeat, they create equanimity and repetition and allow the audience to connect as they listen. You could even call this a melody for a new tune. Improvising is, simply, on-the-spot composing. Try these ideas and then try your own. Remember to keep it simple and use repetition. This type of conversational-style playing will continue into all forms and tunes— something to keep in mind even on more challenging chord progressions.

THE PHINEST BLUES
(Blues)

Roadmap

8 total choruses:
2 choruses of head, 2 choruses of saxophone solo, 2 choruses of piano solo, 2 choruses of head out.

Phineas Newborn, Jr. (1931–1989) was the patriarch of a rich lineage of Memphis-based jazz pianists, with disciples including Harold Mabern, James Williams, Donald Brown, and Mulgrew Miller. Newborn was revered in his time for his exceptional dexterity (often playing complex lines that he would double, two octaves apart, in his left hand) and for the depth of blues feeling that he carried with him into the jazz realm after his early experiences of playing in the bands of artists like Walter Horton and B.B. King.

PHOTO COURTESY OF INSTITUTE OF JAZZ STUDIES, RUTGERS UNIVERSITY

Overview

"The Phinest Blues" was composed as a dedication to Phineas Newborn, Jr., a wonderful and vastly underrated pianist who was equally conversant in deep blues and harmonically sophisticated bebop-based approaches to chord changes. The blues chord progression here is more involved than that in "Bu's Blues," primarily due to the use of turnarounds in measures 8–10. The basic flavor of the blues remains, but there is more of the harmonic complexity associated with modern jazz. Indeed, these kinds of turnarounds are quite typical of a blues played in any kind of jazz context from the bebop era of the mid-1940s onward. The option of playing simple blues vocabulary throughout the song is still there, but it is also worth digging deeper into the changes to take advantage of the added stimulation. The range in tempo for this kind of progression covers virtually the whole spectrum.

Listening Suggestions

Charlie Parker: "Billie's Bounce"

The most influential soloist in modern jazz, Charlie Parker has a vast trove of recordings documenting his playing over this sort of modified blues progression. One of the earliest and best-loved examples of this is his 1945 Savoy recording of "Billie's Bounce"—there are also multiple alternate takes available, which give special insight into his inventiveness.

Dexter Gordon: "Long Tall Dexter"

Tenor saxophonist Dexter Gordon was a prominent soloist for decades, capable of chorus after chorus of fresh material. This 1946 recording catches him very early in his career, alternating between simple blues phrasing and harmonically complex explorations of the chord changes. Also featured on this recording is Bud Powell, the most influential pianist of the bebop era.

Art Blakey: "Now's the Time"

The Charlie Parker songbook became standard fare for generations of jazz musicians exploring this sort of blues progression. Bandleader and drummer Art Blakey was a cohort of Parker's and here offers a lengthy workout on one of Parker's most-played songs, featuring classic bebop-inspired solos by alto saxophonist Lou Donaldson, trumpeter Clifford Brown, and pianist Horace Silver.

Miles Davis: "Straight, No Chaser"

This stretched-out performance from 1958 shows the evolution of bebop with a great variety of approaches, from the technically spectacular wailing of saxophonists John Coltrane and Cannonball Adderley to the sparse, swinging lyricism of trumpeter Davis and pianist Red Garland. The composition is one of the many 12-bar blues songs composed by Thelonious Monk.

Improvising on "The Phinest Blues"

Just like the standard I–IV–V blues, a typical jazz blues consists of 12 measures. You will still want to keep the blues scale as an improvisational option, because it *is* a blues after all.

To add to the blues scale, you can start using the Mixolydian mode (sometimes called the Mixolydian scale, see page 73). You can also use a more *vertical* way of playing. Remember that horizontal playing was using one idea over many chords. Vertical playing is an approach that "spells" each of the chords as they are going by, emphasizing their differences. This is often referred to as "making the changes."

So, for the first four measures of "The Phinest Blues," try playing the following line. It incorporates both the B♭ and C♯ from the blues scale, but notice the sound relies mostly on notes from the Mixolydian mode.

Measures 1–4

When playing over a dominant 7th chord with a Mixolydian mode, try varying your shapes rather than just going up and down the scale. A great way to do this is to move around in 3rds. Try this idea in measures 5–7. Aim to resolve your line when the chord changes back to G7. You can do this by emphasizing the B♭ resolving to a B♮. As you might have noticed, the only difference between the G and C Mixolydian modes is the B♮ in the G7 and the B♭ in the C7. The B♮ is the 3rd of the G7 chord and the B♭ is the 7th of the C7 chord. Both the 3rd and 7th are very important notes in a chord. The 3rd and 7th of a scale or chord define it as major, dominant, or minor. When these notes are emphasized in a solo, this will definitely help to give the impression of "making the changes."

Lastly, notice the ending phrase in the line below. It goes from the 3rd to the root of the G7 chord. The 3rd-to-root movement in a solo always sounds great, especially when played on an offbeat. In this case, the root is played on the "and" of beat 1. To get extra mileage out of playing on the offbeat, add the left hand to accent the rhythm.

Measures 5–7

In measure 8 of the form, we see a big difference between the chords of a simple I–IV–V blues and a jazz blues. The move from Bmin7 to E7 seems like it is out of nowhere, but it isn't at all random. In general, looking ahead to where you are going can be key to knowing exactly where you are. Jazz harmony is no different. As the word "progression" indicates, the chords in a tune are generally going somewhere. Each individual chord has purpose and moves in a specific direction.

In this case, the Amin7 in measure 9 reveals where the Bmin7 and E7 in measure 8 are heading. The movement of Bmin7 to E7 acts as a ii–V going to Amin7. To play over this, you can use E Mixolydian. Notice that the phrase below begins with a pickup leading to measure 8.

Measures 7–9

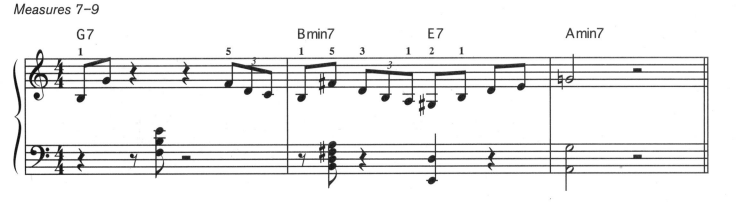

Next, we see that Amin7 goes to D7 and finally to G7. Here, the chords are acting as a ii–V–I7. The example below uses both the 3rds idea and the Mixolydian mode. The phrase ends on the "and" of beat 4, which is accented with a left-hand chord. *Anticipations*—the playing of a note and/or chord a half beat before the expected downbeat—are very effective. Anticipation of the first beat of a measure makes the playing sound more jazz-like. Rhythmic ideas are essential to getting an authentic jazz sound. Playing on the offbeat and, especially, the anticipation of the first beat (the "and" of beat 4) will help you achieve that goal.

Measures 9–11

MR. DEE GEE
(Blues)

Roadmap

8 total choruses:
2 choruses of head, 2 choruses of saxophone solo, 2 choruses of piano solo, 2 choruses of head out.

Overview

"Mr. Dee Gee" is a tribute to the groundbreaking trumpet player and composer Dizzy Gillespie, who was also an accomplished pianist himself. Though not as common as blues progressions based on dominant 7th chords, minor-key 12-bar blues progressions still have a significant place in jazz repertoire, not to mention forming the basis of important blues songs like "Somebody Loan Me a Dime" and "The Thrill Is Gone." Simple blues phrases are particularly compatible with minor blues progressions, as the minor 3rd in the blues scale is well-aligned with the tonality. That said, the relative simplicity of the chords also makes them compatible with more modern, advanced note choices, whether taken from bebop or from the modal vocabularies of artists like John Coltrane. This is also another type of chord progression with a wide range of common tempos, from medium-tempo swing to extremely bright.

Listening Suggestions

Dizzy Gillespie: "Birks' Works"
One of the first significant minor blues tunes to take hold in jazz was this composition by "Mr. Dee Gee" himself. The original studio recording from 1951 features powerhouse solo turns by Gillespie, vibraphonist Milt Jackson, and guitarist Kenny Burrell, but the song became a staple of Gillespie's career and thus there are numerous compelling examples out there.

John Coltrane: "Equinox"
A participant on the original recording of "Birks' Works," tenor saxophonist John Coltrane composed two of the most noteworthy minor blues songs in modern jazz. A year after recording the now-standard "Mr. P.C.," Coltrane debuted his own quartet featuring pianist McCoy Tyner. Those landmark first recording sessions produced "Equinox," a moody but passionate minor blues.

Bill Evans: "Interplay"
The intricacy of this Bill Evans composition camouflages the simple fact that this is a minor blues . . . that is, until the solos come around and the band digs in. Evans plays a flowing solo and offers his signature comping behind trumpeter Freddie Hubbard and guitarist Jim Hall before giving way to bassist Paul Chambers.

Oliver Nelson: "Stolen Moments"
Nelson was a great saxophonist, but he is best known for his authoritative composing and arranging. "Stolen Moments," one of four blues-based songs on the album, also features Eric Dolphy on flute and once again the tandem of Freddie Hubbard on trumpet and Bill Evans on piano. Nelson lengthens the form on the melody before going into a standard 12-bar minor blues for the solos.

Improvising on "Mr. Dee Gee"

When soloing over a minor blues, yet again the blues scale in the corresponding key (in this case, F Minor) works great. Another option is to use a Dorian mode (see page 73) for each of the minor chords. Mixing these two ideas will surely move you well in the direction of making the changes. One way to approach this is to ascend the tones of the appropriate chord (1–♭3–5–♭7) then descend the Dorian mode, like below.

This time, try the opposite approach: ascend the scale and descend the chord.

Now, start on the 3rd and ascend the chord to the 9th, and then come down the scale. This will not only start the phrase in a new place but also end the phrase in a new way. This one is over the iv chord.

Now, let's take the same idea and try it with a different chord voicing implied by the arpeggio. Ascend the new voicing, repeat it, and then descend the scale. This is essentially the same idea using different inversions of the chord.

Practicing this approach can be great for your playing, because in order to solo with fluency, you will need to master your scales and chords. Remember to establish and reinforce comfortable fingerings, as that can hold a pianist back when it comes to improvising. It is very important to work on a piece of music until your fingering is solid.

Another approach to playing over a minor blues is to focus on a minor pentatonic scale (see page 72). This will be similar to the approach taken on the previous page, but a bit easier and a little hipper at the same time.

F Minor Pentatonic can be used over the whole progression (another horizontal approach) and has a very open sound. Following is a way to use it over the last six measures of the progression. The ♭5 (the only note from the F Blues scale not also in the F Minor Pentatonic) is added over the D♭7 to make the phrase even better, due to the compatibility of that note with that chord.

Measures 7–12

You can also approach the dominant chords in measures 9–10 by using the corresponding Mixolydian modes and resolving to the pentatonic scale. This is very similar to the above approach, except in this case, the E♮ is added over the C7. This use of the 3rd more clearly defines the chord as a C7. Notice there is a ♭9 and ♯5 on the C7 chord, and those notes are reflected in the right hand as well. Using scale alterations is a great way to add color to the chord, and in this situation, it actually makes the transition smoother when going from the V to the i chord.

Measures 9–12

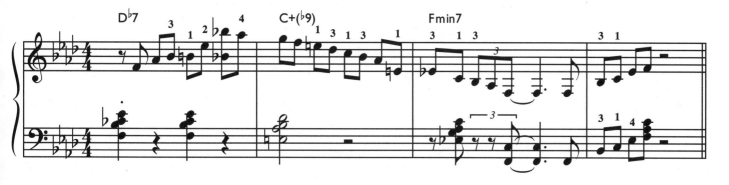

BOPPIN' WITH J-MAC
(Bebop)

Roadmap

6 total choruses:
1 chorus of head, 2 choruses of saxophone solo, 2 choruses of piano solo, 1 chorus of
head out.

Overview

"Boppin' with J-Mac" is a tribute to Jackie McLean, who was a great saxophonist, composer, and pioneer of jazz education. The chord changes here are most closely associated with the old-time jazz tune "Sweet Georgia Brown," though it has been recycled many times on tunes like "Dig," "Bright Mississippi," and "Sweet Clifford." These chords revolve around a dominant cycle, a series of dominant 7th chords that resolve to one another in a sort of harmonic chain reaction. The stimulation provided by these chords (due to the use of the cycle, a soloist can't simply stay in a single key for very long) has made them very popular among bebop-influenced musicians, though there are great examples from the swing era as well. There are some good medium-tempo examples, but tunes with these chords are most typically played fast.

Listening Suggestions

The King Cole Trio: "Sweet Georgia Brown"

As bebop was in its infancy in the 1940s, Nat King Cole's trio helped bridge the gap, using many of the devices associated with swing-era music yet possessing the fluency associated with the bebop greats. While best known for his vocals, Cole was a tremendously important pianist. His solo work and that of guitarist Oscar Moore stand out on their fast-moving rendition of this tune.

Bud Powell: "Sweet Georgia Brown"

Taking the baton from Cole, pianist Powell offers a clinic here in what bebop piano is about. Propelled by Max Roach's drums, the tempo is blisteringly fast. Powell keeps his left hand simple and fills in all the gaps with aggressive, flowing solo lines in his right hand. It's no wonder that he was the most-imitated pianist in jazz for years.

Miles Davis: "Dig"

Saxophonists Jackie McLean and Sonny Rollins were both only 20 when they participated on trumpeter Miles Davis's classic recording of McLean's tune "Dig." Youth notwithstanding, they both display the sort of fluency that became expected of bebop-minded saxophonists to follow Charlie Parker. Miles and J-Mac would go on to re-record a slower version of the song under the title "Donna."

Thelonious Monk: "Bright Mississippi"

One of numerous unique things about pianist and composer Thelonious Monk's place in jazz history is that he came of age as a participant in the bebop movement but his own musical style is rather different from that of his contemporary Bud Powell, or indeed any other bebopper. His angular, quirky style of comping and soloing is on full display in this spirited performance.

Improvising on "Boppin' with J-Mac"

In this tune, the chords start out moving in 4ths similar to a blues, but with a slower *harmonic rhythm* (the rate at which chords change). At the beginning, each chord is played for four measures, which is a lot of time for one chord. Instead of solely relying on a blues scale or even the Mixolydian mode (though both will work nicely) let's superimpose another chord over the progression. Pianists do this all the time in order to change the tonality of the chord progression, especially when the chord is one you have to stay on for more than two measures.

To do this, try adding a Cmin7 over the F7 chord in the first four measures. Cmin7 is a good choice because it typically precedes the dominant chord (F7) in the common ii–V–I progression. An example of this would be to start with Cmin7 for one measure, then go to F7 for one measure, then back to Cmin7, and again to F7. Remember, all the while, the bass will be playing the F7 chord underneath this. This will create a suspended sound, which will add a lot of interest to what could otherwise run the risk of being a slightly monotonous plateau. The scales for Cmin7 and F7 use the exact same notes, but they are slightly different chords. When you go from Cmin7 to F7, the 7th of Cmin7 (B♭) has to drop a half step to become the 3rd of F7 (A). (This holds true for the same progression in other keys as well.)

Pay close attention to how the chords/scales are played in the following example. Notice in particular where the Cmin7 is being spelled out.

Measures 1–4

Notice there is an E♮ in the previous example. This note is not *diatonic* (does not belong) to Cmin7 or F7, but it is part of the bebop scale (see page 74). Since this chord progression comes out of the bebop era, this is a perfect place to use the bebop scale. A bebop scale adds an extra note to another scale (for instance, a major or minor scale) so that the chord tones are played on the downbeats.

There are some commonly used bebop scales like the one used above over the F7, which adds a half step between the root and ♭7 (in this case, the added tone is E♮). Below, we have the same scale (this time in B♭) over the next few chords as well.

Measures 5–8

The last five measures of the song are a little more challenging to maneuver because of how fast the chords are moving. Although the chord motion is pretty straightforward, two beats is never a lot of time to clearly state a chord change. It will be important to use the most important notes of each chord, particularly the 3rd and 7th. Start by spelling the chords like this:

Measures 20–24

To connect the chord progression with greater fluidity, try looking for the closest chord tone of the next chord. For example, on B♭7, when you get to the note A♭ (7th), go to G (3rd of E♭7) and move down from there. Similarly, when on the A♭7 chord, play the G♭ (7th) and then move to the F (7th of G7). Continue with this idea.

Measures 20–24

Now try adding in the Mixolydian modes and bebop scales. This takes a little more maneuvering because scales can become vague if you are not choosing good notes. Aim for 3rds or 7ths and you will be in better shape.

Measures 20–24

Lastly, varying the rhythm will add new life to the same line.

Measures 20–24

TOMMY'S TOUCH
(Standard Changes)

Roadmap

6 total choruses:
1 chorus of head, 2 choruses of saxophone solo, 2 choruses of piano solo, 1 chorus of
head out.

Overview

"Tommy's Touch" was composed as a tribute to the great Detroit pianist Tommy Flanagan, a participant in classic recordings by a host of artists including Sonny Rollins, John Coltrane, and Ella Fitzgerald. The changes are inspired by the jazz standard "Autumn Leaves," which is a stellar example of how a song can go back and forth between a major key and its relative minor. That song was traditionally played as a ballad in the key of E Minor (or G Major, depending on how you look at it) and in some settings still is. However, with the evolution of this set of changes as a vehicle for jazz performance, modern-day protocols are that the tempo is generally medium swing and the key is generally G Minor (or B-flat Major).

Listening Suggestions

Cannonball Adderley: "Autumn Leaves"
Trumpeter Miles Davis made no secret for his admiration of pianist Ahmad Jamal. "Autumn Leaves" is one of numerous Jamal arrangements that Miles adapted for his own performances. While pianist Hank Jones and nominal bandleader Cannonball Adderley on alto saxophone are both prominently featured, this classic performance bears the strong stamp of the Harmon-muted Davis sound.

Bill Evans Trio: "Autumn Leaves"
The Bill Evans Trio with Scott LaFaro and Paul Motian was a game-changing ensemble in terms of the level of interplay one could expect within a rhythm section or trio, all the more remarkable considering that LaFaro's tragic death cut the collaboration short after less than two years. "Autumn Leaves" is one of the most influential and hard-swinging tracks from their shared catalog.

Bobby Timmons: "Autumn Leaves"
Bobby Timmons is sometimes pigeonholed as a "funky" pianist due to the bluesy, hard-swinging performances and songs for which he is best known. While that characterization is indeed unfair in the sense of painting a limited picture of his diverse skills, there's no shame in swinging hard and he and his trio do precisely that on this super-tight live performance.

Wynton Marsalis: "Autumn Leaves"
Wynton Marsalis is part of an extremely musical family. While he is best-known for work that is adherent to older jazz traditions, he has been responsible for some cutting-edge work himself. This version of "Autumn Leaves" revolves around unusual rhythmic twists and turns and the slashing, up-tempo groove played by the rhythm section of Marcus Roberts, Robert Hurst, and Jeff "Tain" Watts.

Improvising on "Tommy's Touch"

Before starting any piece, it is always a good idea to figure out how the chord progression is laid out. This will help you understand the form and how to approach the improvisation. This standard chord progression is made up of two related keys. In the first four measures, the chords move to the key of B♭ Major using a ii–V–I progression. Then, the key changes to the relative minor, G Minor, via a minor ii⌀–V–i. Notice how, with only slight variations, the rest of the song continues in this pattern of either ii–V–I in B♭ Major or ii⌀–V–i in G Minor.

A way to approach a major ii–V–I is to play through the modes (see page 73). Let's use C Dorian on the Cmin7, F Mixolydian on the F7, and B♭ Ionian (B♭ Major) on the B♭Maj7. Then, we'll use E♭ Lydian on the IV chord, E♭Maj7. Note that all of these modes are derived from the key of B♭ Major.

Now, try using the arpeggiated chords and diatonic scales in the manner we discussed when looking at "Boppin' with J-Mac."

Here is another way to approach it. The example below is almost the same line, but there is added variety to the rhythm as well as non-diatonic notes (notes outside the key). Specifically, the note G♭ over an F7 creates a ♭9 and the note A♭ is the ♯9. These tones add extra color to a dominant chord that resolves to a I chord. When these chord alterations are added, it is helpful to reflect these changes in your left hand.

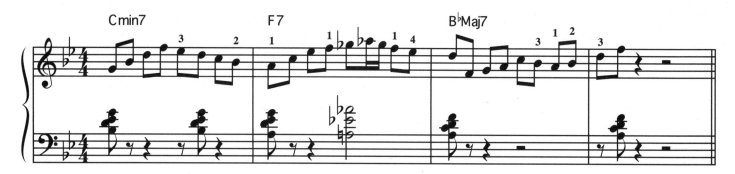

The idea of playing over a minor ii⌀–V–i is slightly different than the major ii–V–I. The main difference begins with the quality of the chords. Instead of just a simple minor 7th for the ii chord, we now have a min7♭5 (or half-diminished ⌀) chord. The dominant chord is usually played here as an altered dominant (that is, with some combination of ♭5 or ♯5 and/or ♭9 or ♯9). Additionally, instead of ending on a major chord, it ends on a minor chord.

Often, students of jazz piano are confused as to what to do over a half-diminished chord. It is easier to think of this chord as being grouped with the other chords—half-diminished chords are rarely seen on their own. They are mostly used in the minor ii⌀–V–i progression.

In this progression, using a harmonic minor scale (see page 72) can work really well. So if the chords are Amin7♭5–D7♭9–Gmin7, use a G Harmonic Minor scale. Remember, using one scale over a group of chords is known as the horizontal approach.

Now, let's mix in a bit of vertical thinking as we switch the F♯ from the harmonic minor scale (F♯ is the 3rd of D7) to an F♮ when we get to Gmin7 (F♮ is the ♭7th of Gmin7).

This last example still features the notes of the harmonic minor scale, but on the D7 chord, we will also use an F♮ (a note belonging to G Dorian), which creates a ♯9 over the D7. The phrase played over D7 creates a D7 with a ♭9 and a ♯9. This is a really colorful sound and is useful when you want to flex your jazz prowess.

Try putting all these lines and ideas into Tommy's Touch. Your solos will be taking off in no time!

BLUES FOR BIRD
(Blues)

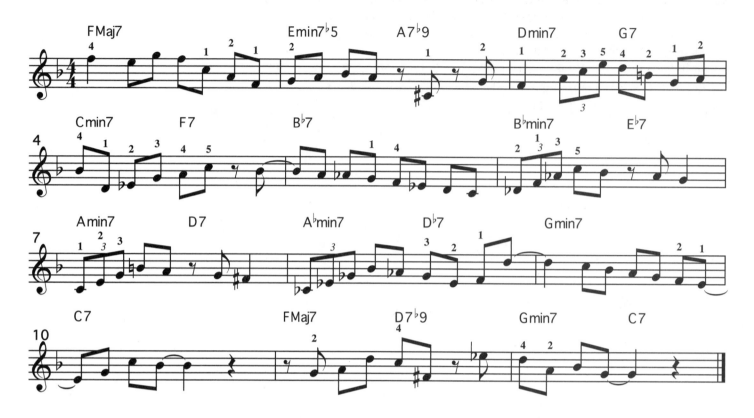

Roadmap

10 total choruses:
2 choruses of head, 3 choruses of saxophone solo, 3 choruses of piano solo, 2 choruses of head out.

*Alto saxophone virtuoso **Charlie Parker** (1920–1955) was the most influential musician of the bebop movement, indeed considered by most to be second only to Louis Armstrong in the lexicon of groundbreaking soloists in jazz history. In his tragically short life, he established much of the vocabulary that is at the foundation of jazz as we know it.*

PHOTO COURTESY OF INSTITUTE OF JAZZ STUDIES, RUTGERS UNIVERSITY

Overview

"Blues for Bird" is one of virtually countless musical tributes that have been made over the years to saxophonist Charlie "Yardbird" Parker. One thing that Bird pioneered was the further expansion of what a blues progression could be. There are several variations on what is sometimes called "Bird blues," but the general protocol is that the first measure still has the I chord and the fifth measure still has the IV chord (with, more often than not, the I chord returning on measure 11). The remaining measures are generally saturated with chords cycling through with minimal respite from the motion; while standard blues devices can still apply, there is a much greater demand for "making the changes." This sort of progression was a response to advanced bebop musicians' desire to have greater stimulation from the songs they used for improvisation. The tempos tend to be anywhere in the medium-to-fast range, most often somewhere in the realm of "medium-up."

Listening Suggestions

Miles Davis: "Sippin' at Bells"
Miles Davis puts his hat in the ring of heavily modified blues tunes on this cut from a 1947 recording session, the first of his long career as a bandleader. The recording features solos by Miles, pianist John Lewis (later to become the leader of The Modern Jazz Quartet), and Charlie Parker himself, making a comparatively rare appearance on tenor saxophone.

Bud Powell: "Dance of the Infidels"
Both in the complexity of the chord changes and in the fluid, bebop-rooted solo lines played by Powell on the piano, this piece is a good bit removed from what most people think of as blues. This recording also features trumpeter Fats Navarro, tenor saxophonist Sonny Rollins, and drummer Roy Haynes, all young players who would become influential themselves.

Charlie Parker: "Blues for Alice"
This is the best-known song in this modified blues (or "Bird blues") style. Parker is, unsurprisingly, completely at ease with the increased complexity of the chords compared to other blues tunes of his like "Now's the Time" or "Billie's Bounce." Trumpeter Red Rodney and, once again, pianist John Lewis also get solo turns in before they return to Bird's challenging melody.

Roland Kirk: "Blues for Alice"
Multi-instrumentalist Roland Kirk did a good bit of experimental music in his career but here offers a relatively traditional take on "Blues for Alice," buoyed by the swinging rhythm section of Richard Wyands, Art Davis, and Charlie Persip. Kirk plays multiple saxophones on this track (sometimes at the same time!), soloing authoritatively on tenor and on the soprano-like manzello.

Improvising on "Blues for Bird"

When playing over dense blues changes, we should consider the many options for improvisation. For this tune, let's analyze how the blues scale, harmonic minor, and bebop scales can all be used. Below, the solo is broken into pieces to explain what is happening, but it could easily be put together to use as a whole chorus of soloing.

In the first measure, we are spelling out an FMaj7 chord using a *syncopated* rhythm (emphasizing the offbeats), a great way to start a solo. Then for the Emin7♭5 to A7 (a ii∅–V in D Minor), a D Harmonic Minor scale is used.

The one note difference in this measure is the F♯, which can be thought of as a *passing tone* (a non-diatonic tone used to connect two diatonic tones). Using passing tones or bebop scales (which, as we've learned, add passing tones to existing scales or modes) are helpful when the chords are not lining up for the sound you want or just to add extra color. In this phrase, the line is working toward the next chord, Dmin7. Watch how the line directs you right to the 5th of Dmin7.

Measures 1–3

Now that we have landed on the Dmin7, check out the pattern that is coming up. In measures 3 and 4 we have a Dmin7–G7 to a Cmin7–F7. In the big picture, this continues the gravitational pull of the chord progression, but also, these are both simply ii–V's one whole step apart. Therefore, whatever you do in one key can be transposed and recreated in the next key. Throughout this whole progression, there are many chord patterns that repeat. Sometimes, the chords are the same, just moved down a half or whole step. When this occurs, it is effective to adapt the same line to the next key. Repetition of a phrase gives the listener something to connect with, especially in such a dense chord progression. Try it below.

Measures 3–4

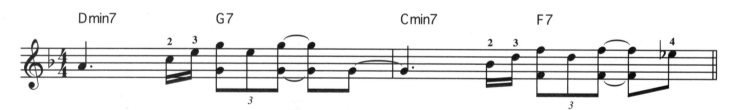

In measures 5–8, the repetition continues using a dominant bebop scale (see page 74), in which a half step is added between the root and ♭7th. When playing a dominant bebop scale, it is best to play these notes successively (the root, ♮7, and ♭7th). Note that the appropriate dominant bebop scale, with the same root as the V chord, can be used over the whole ii–V. So, over B♭min7–E♭7, use only the E♭ Dominant Bebop scale followed by the D and D♭ Dominant Bebop scales on the subsequent measures.

Measures 5–8

The last four measures use the C Dominant Bebop scale over Gmin7–C7 and then a bit of the blues scale on the turnaround in the last measure.

Measures 9–12

Here is a second chorus of the blues in the same vein. Try to identify all the same elements. Remember to look for the harmonic minor scale over the minor ii∅–V, the bebop dominant scale over dominant chords, and notes from the blues scale.

SEPARATION ANXIETY
(Standard Changes)

Roadmap

6 total choruses:
1 chorus of head, 2 choruses of saxophone solo, 2 choruses of piano solo, 1 chorus of head out.

Overview

"Separation Anxiety" uses a set of chords in the style of the standard "Alone Together," which presents a couple of important but less common challenges to jazz musicians. One is that the song is primarily in the key of D Minor, when the majority of commonly played songs in jazz are either in major keys or in blues-based tonalities. It also goes through several temporary modulations that require improvisers to be on their toes. The other challenge is in the asymmetry of the form. Most songs in jazz (and indeed most in this book) are based on 12-bar blues forms or the piecing together of 8-measure sections (most often putting four of them into a 32-bar song). Examination of these changes reveals two 14-bar sections followed by two 8-bar sections. While "Alone Together" was initially most often played as a ballad, this has evolved over time. Nowadays, these changes are typically played with a swing feel and at a medium tempo.

Listening Suggestions

Jim Hall and Ron Carter: "Alone Together"
One of the great duos in modern jazz history was bassist Ron Carter's collaboration with guitarist Jim Hall, and "Alone Together" was a most appropriate title track to their first album together. They both play with great subtlety, showing command of time, space and silence rather than using an endless stream of notes to cover up the absence of drums or piano.

Stanley Turrentine: "Alone Together"
There is a short list of artists in modern jazz whose musical personalities are considered to be virtually synonymous with blues-inflected, hard-swinging music. Tenor saxophonist Stanley Turrentine and pianist Gene Harris (leader of The Three Sounds) are certainly on this list, so it is not at all surprising that this performance swings with finger-popping swagger.

Art Farmer: "Alone Together"
The facile and lyrical trumpeter Art Farmer (heard here on flugelhorn) teams up with the super-tight rhythm section of Cedar Walton, Sam Jones, and Billy Higgins. Jones, Farmer, and Walton all get lengthy solo turns. As you listen, notice not only the fluency of the soloists, but also the level of interplay among the musicians.

Lee Konitz: "Variations on Alone Together"
This is a fascinating tour-de-force by the innovative saxophonist Lee Konitz. Over the course of 15 minutes, he interprets the song alone, in duets with drummer Elvin Jones, vibraphonist Karl Berger, and bassist Eddie Gomez, and then in a free-wheeling quartet with all three of these musicians. There are many experimental components here, but "Alone Together" keeps coming back.

Improvising on "Separation Anxiety"

Though this song seems to have many chord changes, it can be simplified. The A section (measures 1–14) cycles around in D Minor for five measures before going to G Minor via a minor iiø–V–i. Then, the Gmin7, which is functioning as a i, turns into a ii chord heading to FMaj7. This is not a strange transition because the chords all belong to the key of D Minor, which is the relative minor of F Major. As such, the tonality really has not changed much.

The more challenging thing about the ending of this section is the transition to D Major, as well as its short duration (only two measures). Landing on the DMaj7 sounds dramatic, especially as it returns to D Minor at the top. Anytime a composer goes from a major to a minor (or vice versa) with the same tonic (known as *parallel major* and *parallel minor*), it adds a lot of emotion.

The harmonic minor scale is usually a good choice for playing over a minor iiø–V–i. As such, we'll use D and G Harmonic Minor, corresponding with the iiø–V–i progressions in those keys. Notice where the line approaches the Dmin7 in measure 5—this is a good place to try a larger jump in intervals. In order to avoid the dryness of just running through scales, make sure your lines sound like they are headed somewhere specific. Ending a scale with a larger interval produces an intentional, effective sound—like that was where you were planning to go with the scale. However, if trying to play the changes and express a tonality, jumping around with large intervals will not do the trick.

In the following example, notice the clear stating of the D Minor and a clear statement of harmonic minor tonality over the Emin7♭5–A7♭9, which all leads to the Dmin7 in the fifth measure.

Measures 1–7

The A section continues by going to F Major by means of Bmin7–E7 and then, more traditionally, Gmin7–C7. This section ends a little deceptively; the chords sound like they should resolve to D Minor, but instead, they resolve to D Major. Making this clear in your solo is important, so it is critical to play an F♯ over the DMaj7.

Measures 9–13

The bridge (or B section, measures 15–22) gives the soloist an opportunity to change up the musical ideas a bit. In this song, all of the chords found in the bridge are already in the A section, so there is a greater need to make a clear change in the solo. One way to do this is to incorporate chords into melodic lines. When playing chords, the top note is the note that will sound as the melody. It is important to think "top down" as you create this type of chordal melody, conceiving a melody and then harmonizing underneath. Following is an example of a melodic single-line solo for the B section.

Measures 15–23

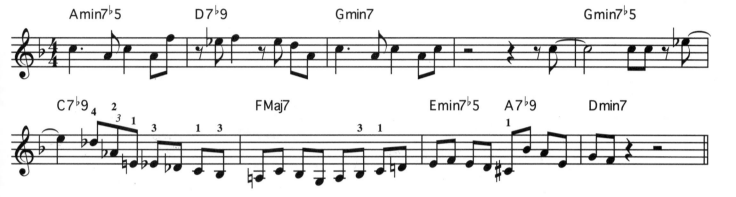

This perfectly good line could be beefed up a bit to add more interest. Depth can be added by playing notes under some of the stronger beats. The notes you choose are up to you, but a good place to start is to add notes from the chords.

Over the first measure, the strong beats for this phrase are beats 1, 3, and the "and" of 4. Adding a rootless voicing (see page 76) underneath that note will sound good, but there is also quite a bit of space between the chord and the melody note. Using a 4th below the melody in the right hand as well will fill in that space. For the example, below, the chords are only played where the melody should be accented. This gives the phrase an extra kick that it wouldn't have without that reinforcement.

Measures 15–20

GOLDEN SILVER
(Bebop/Rhythm Changes)

D.C. al Fine
(2nd ending only)

Roadmap

6 total choruses:
1 chorus of head, 2 choruses of saxophone solo, 2 choruses of piano solo, 1 chorus of
head out.

Overview

A dedication to pianist and composer Horace Silver, "Golden Silver" adds one more to the vast trove of *rhythm changes* songs in jazz. That term refers to songs using variations on the chord progression first used by George Gershwin in the song "I Got Rhythm." Rhythm changes are second only to blues among the most common chord progressions in jazz. In addition to the original Gershwin tune, the list of these songs includes "Lester Leaps In," "Moose the Mooche," "Rhythm-A-Ning," "Room 608," "The Eternal Triangle," the theme from "The Flintstones," and the songs cited below, among many others. Most typically played at faster tempos, these changes occur in a 32-bar AABA form. The main challenge in the A sections is the rate at which the chords move, although for the most part, the chords refer back to a single tonal center. The bridge (B section), meanwhile, revolves around a dominant cycle like the one we navigated in "Boppin' with J-Mac."

Listening Suggestions

Benny Goodman: "I Got Rhythm"
This influential performance of "I Got Rhythm" was recorded live at a landmark concert at New York's Carnegie Hall. Clarinetist Goodman is best-known for his big band, but is heard here with his influential quartet, which in the mid-1930s broke the color barrier for live jazz ensembles. Goodman, pianist Teddy Wilson, vibraphonist Lionel Hampton, and drummer Gene Krupa are all featured.

Charlie Parker and Dizzy Gillespie: "Shaw 'Nuff"
The bebop movement embraced rhythm changes as a vehicle for advanced improvisation, and as the movement's two most prominent figures, it is not surprising that both saxophonist Charlie Parker and trumpeter Dizzy Gillespie wrote multiple tunes with these chords. This is one of the first, and the technical and harmonic virtuosity they display in their solos and the unison melody is stunning.

Miles Davis: "Oleo"
This is the one of the most commonly played rhythm changes in modern jazz. The original version (from the *Bags' Groove* album) features saxophonist Sonny Rollins (the song's composer) and pianist Horace Silver. Miles went on to record it on multiple other occasions, featuring saxophonists John Coltrane, Cannonball Adderley, and Hank Mobley and pianists Red Garland, Bill Evans, and Wynton Kelly.

James Moody: "Anthropology"
With a chord progression so common, it stands to reason that it will be adapted in various ways over time. While James Moody is best known for his work in the bebop vein, he and pianist Kenny Barron incorporate elements of modal jazz and other less-typical sounds into this high-octane 1973 version of Charlie Parker's "Anthropology."

Rhythm changes have a standard form that will give a performer many needed skills for other tunes. Performers able to play over these changes comfortably will inevitably be able to play over many other jazz progressions as well.

Improvising on "Golden Silver"

Spelling the chords and using bebop scales are still effective tools here. Now, however, we will add some new sounds by applying the diminished scale (see page 75). The diminished scale can be used over most dominant chords, and this use is very effective because we hear not only the chord tones but also some hip upper extensions. Notice that a diminished scale used on a dominant chord is not the same as a diminished scale used on a diminished chord. Instead of a whole step/half step construction, use a "half-whole" diminished scale. Here it is over a G7.

Notice the scale above includes the chord tones G, B, D, and F, as well as the 13 (E). Played over a dominant chord, this diminished scale also includes the ♭9, #9, and #11. These altered chord tones sound amazing over the resolving dominant 7th chords.

Try it out! During the A section, there isn't enough time to play the whole diminished scale over the dominant 7th chords, so small, decisive parts will work better, as demonstrated in the following example.

Next, we'll focus on the chord tones from the diminished scale. On the G7 in the first measure, the 3rd, 5th, 7th, and ♭9th are played. This line leads nicely into the 5th (G) of the Cmin7 in the second measure. Then, the same thing is done on the F7 going to Dmin7. The third and fourth measures use a similar idea.

In the fifth measure, use a simple, bluesy phrase. In the following measure, clearly spell out E♭Maj7 and A♭7. Choosing notes like the 3rd and/or 7th articulates the harmony more clearly when the chords are passing by quickly.

Instead of playing a diminished chord straight up or down, try breaking it up. This is sometimes called a broken-chord approach. Try to listen for this sound when you are checking out jazz greats playing on rhythm changes—you will hear it often. Below, let's use the broken-chord approach over the whole A section.

When finishing up the A section, notice the different endings. Being able to distinguish between the two is important for getting the most out of the chords. The first ending brings you back to the top of the progression, so the lines should sound like they are heading back to B♭ Major. Using a turnaround like the one below will help this happen.

For the second ending, try to resolve the phrase on the B♭Maj7 before you start heading to the bridge.

In the bridge, we are once again moving in 4ths, as in "Boppin' with J-Mac"; so the same ideas used for that tune can be used here, including turning the dominant chords into ii–V's, aiming for the 3rds and 7ths of the chords, and using the bebop and diminished scales.

To add to these ideas, try putting upper extensions into play, especially the ♯11. This gives the dominant chords a real open, modern sound. A way to add the ♯11 is to think of the major triad one whole step above the chord you are on. In other words, on the D7, think of an E Major triad. Below, the chords are notated with the 3rd and 7th of each chord on the bottom and the appropriate triad on top.

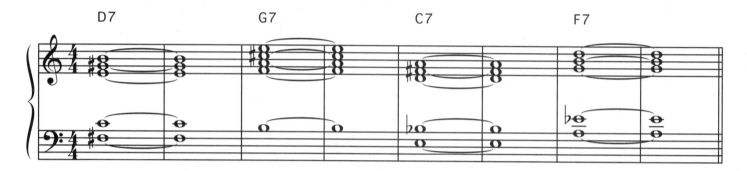

Here is the same idea, but with better voice leading.

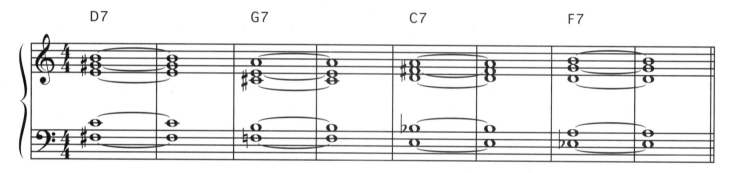

Now, try arpeggiating the triads up and down. Note that where you start and how high you go determines where you land. You always want to be mindful of where you are going. Try looking ahead and aiming for a specific chord tone of the chord to which you are resolving.

Playing these triads up and down and in inversions will create a really modern sound. This is especially true when you alternate these triads with the triads built from the roots of those chords. For example, on D7, alternate between a D Major triad and an E Major triad.

Modern sound:

The triad can also be added into a traditional bebop-style solo in the B section.

More traditional, straight-ahead sound:

DESTINATION MILES
(Waltz)

Roadmap

6 total choruses:

1 chorus of head, 2 choruses of saxophone solo, 2 choruses of piano solo, 1 chorus of head out.

Overview

"Destination Miles" provides us with our first exposure in this book to time signatures other than $\frac{4}{4}$. Jazz songs in $\frac{3}{4}$ time are generally referred to as *jazz waltzes*, even though technically the rhythm is generally not what might inspire someone to dance a traditional waltz! The removal of the symmetry attached to having four beats in a measure opens up multiple rhythmic possibilities. It also demands that the musicians adapt their content to accommodate the time change, since $\frac{4}{4}$ cliches won't fit anymore.

There are three typical ways of feeling a song in $\frac{3}{4}$ time, each relevant to different musical intentions. One is to emphasize every quarter note, just as one might on any other swinging tune. Another is to emphasize the dotted quarter note, thus dividing the three-beat measure in half. Yet another is to play "in one" and emphasize only the first beat of each measure (the dotted half note), creating a more ethereal feeling. The chords here are inspired by the classic song "Someday My Prince Will Come."

Listening Suggestions

Dave Brubeck: "Someday My Prince Will Come"
Pianist Dave Brubeck is best known for his body of work experimenting with the world outside of $\frac{4}{4}$ time; given how commonplace waltzes now are in jazz, it is noteworthy that before Brubeck (as well as drummer Max Roach), $\frac{3}{4}$ was considered an "odd" time signature. Saxophonist Paul Desmond (who composed "Take Five," the Brubeck Quartet's best-loved performance) is prominently featured here.

Miles Davis: "Someday My Prince Will Come"
Starting in the late 1950s, Miles Davis recorded a number of diverse-sounding songs in $\frac{3}{4}$ such as "All Blues," "Circle," "Footprints," and "Iris," but this infectious track from 1960 remains his most popular waltz and debatably the standard rendition of this song in jazz. Pianist Wynton Kelly and tenor saxophonists Hank Mobley and John Coltrane all get authoritative solo turns here.

Bill Evans: "Someday My Prince Will Come"
The Bill Evans Trio with Scott LaFaro and Paul Motian innovated substantially in the realm of rhythmic flexibility for a jazz ensemble, but due to LaFaro's premature death, there are few examples of their treatment of songs in $\frac{3}{4}$ time. As such, this subtle performance from their first recording together is a particularly important document.

Sonny Stitt and Don Patterson: "Someday My Prince Will Come"
Saxophonist Sonny Stitt and organist Don Patterson were both known for their total mastery of the bebop idiom (indeed, Stitt was considered one of Charlie Parker's musical heirs) and for their ability to meld that with the sound of the blues. That they are able to seamlessly inject all of this into this performance is indicative of how common $\frac{3}{4}$ time had become in jazz by 1965.

Playing in "three" is just like any other time signature in that feeling the beat will be easier the more you do it. As far as comping goes, it is important for a pianist to know what the drummer and bass player are doing in order to fit in. Following are some examples of different ways to comp in "three." Note that the chord voicings are the same for each example, it is just the feel that changes. These different feels can change within a song. It is important to have open ears to hear what the rest of the rhythm section is doing. For example, the song could start in one feel and move to another and then back again.

The example below shows a comping pattern to use for a dotted-half-note feel.

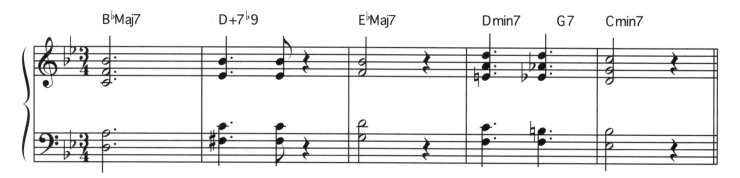

Here is a comping pattern with a strong "three" feel (that is, emphasizing each quarter note). Usually, this type of feel kicks in when the bass starts walking in $\frac{3}{4}$.

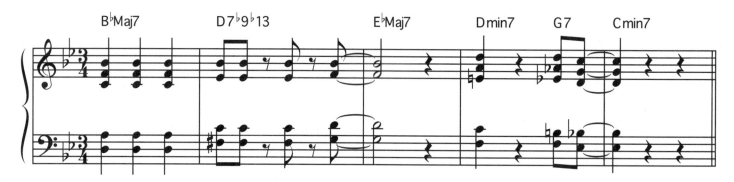

This next one can be used in any of the feels but will work nicely with a strong beat on "one."

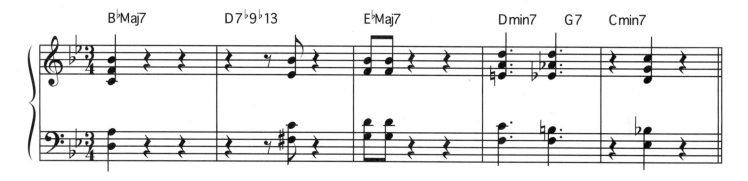

A great technique for soloing on this tune (or any piece of music) is to use a *motif*, which is a short musical idea that can be used as a jumping-off point. A motif can be rhythmic or melodic or both. Once a motif is played it can be repeated either exactly or transposed from the original key. Usually, these small ideas will lead to other ideas, thus developing the solo. There is no right or wrong way to do this. The main point to playing a motif is to help a soloist start a solo with a clear idea.

The following example of a motif begins in the first measure with a D, G, and F. This intervallic and rhythmic idea repeats in the second and third measures but now using notes that fit the appropriate chords. By measure 4, the motif starts to morph into a new idea by changing where in the measure it is placed; it now begins on beat 3 instead of beat 1. Soon after, the motif has other notes surrounding it until the musical idea goes somewhere else. By measure 9, another motif is introduced. That motif also morphs and eventually leads the musical phrase to its end.

Roadmap

5 total choruses:

1 chorus of head, 1 chorus of saxophone solo, 2 choruses of piano solo, 1 chorus of head out.

SITTING IN: JAZZ PIANO   **45**

Overview

"Carob Powder" is a tune with chord changes in the style of Ray Noble's "Cherokee." This is one of the signature chord progressions of modern jazz and particularly of bebop. Indeed, until John Coltrane came up with "Giant Steps" in 1959 (see "It Takes Big Feet" later in this book), these changes were widely considered to be the biggest test to a musician's virtuosity. There are a couple reasons for this. One is that the tempo is usually extremely fast—you needn't start there by any means, but these changes are fairly often played at a tempo exceeding 300 beats per minute. The other significant challenge is that the B section (bridge) of the song modulates every four measures, and into keys that are remote from the "home" key in the A section. That said, while the challenges are substantial, they are not mysterious—they just require practice!

Listening Suggestions

Charlie Parker: "Koko"
Though he also recorded "Cherokee" early in his career, the 1945 recording of "Koko" is the most prominent example of alto saxophonist Parker soloing over these changes. After a short opening melody statement alongside Dizzy Gillespie, he dives right into the changes and unleashes a stream of flowing, inventive lines that have inspired generations of beboppers since then to learn and incorporate them into their vocabulary.

Don Byas: "Cherokee"
Don Byas was one of the first major tenor saxophonists of the bebop movement and he eats up the chord changes on this performance of "Cherokee." Particularly interesting here is that the rhythm section plays at a still-bright but fairly relaxed tempo, while, in his solo, Byas consistently plays in double-time, foreshadowing extreme tempos that would follow in the ensuing years.

Bud Powell: "Cherokee"
Many have compared Bud Powell's impact on pianists to that of Charlie Parker on saxophonists. In any case, he was certainly "the cat" among bop pianists and this trio track with Ray Brown and Max Roach is one of his signature performances of the late 1940s. His solo lines here are authoritative both rhythmically and harmonically.

Clifford Brown/Max Roach Quintet: "Cherokee"
A year and a half before this 1955 recording, Clifford Brown recorded a powerful version of "Cherokee" with Art Blakey on drums. Here, with drummer and co-leader Roach, Brown shows otherworldly fluency as he makes this song and this tempo sound completely relaxed. The other soloists here are saxophonist Harold Land and pianist Richie Powell (Bud's younger brother).

Improvising on "Carob Powder"

When playing a fast song like this, the options for soloing become a little more limited. There are two great ways to approach playing fast. The first is this: go slow! Starting at a slower tempo when beginning to practice allows a soloist the time needed to teach the fingers to maneuver through changes fluently. If time is not given to slow practice, playing smooth eighth-note lines will be impossible, mostly because it takes time to figure out good fingering.

Once able to play a line smoothly at a slow tempo, gradually increase the speed. Move in small increments to get the best results. The use of a metronome can be really helpful here.

Practice like this brings not only fluidity but also a level of comfort that is needed when the changes are moving fast. Just like a runner needs to be relaxed as he sprints, a pianist's fingers need to be relaxed in order to move quickly. So, remember as you practice slowly to make sure the fingers are staying limber, not tight or clenched.

Below is a passage to practice for fluidity over the A section. The altered scale (see page 74) is used over the resolving dominant 7th chords: the B♭7 in measure 4 and the F7 in measure 14. The altered scale gives these chords a thicker sound because it includes the ♭9, ♯9, ♭5, and ♯5 of those chords. With these tones, your jazz vocabulary will explode! Try it out below, starting at a slow tempo.

Measures 1–15

The second thing to try when playing a quick tempo is to keep things simple. This can be done by maintaining a simple melodic line or by consolidating chords. To retain rhythmic and melodic simplicity, try to keep the right-hand notes within an octave to prevent the fingers from having to cross too much (if at all).

Measures 17–19

Notice in the next eight measures the line only implies motion from V to I instead of making all the notes of the ii–V–I. This simplified way of playing a ii–V–I takes the pressure off fitting a bunch of notes into a small amount of time. Plus, these lines stay in a close position, which makes it easier for the hand to move quickly.

Measures 21–28

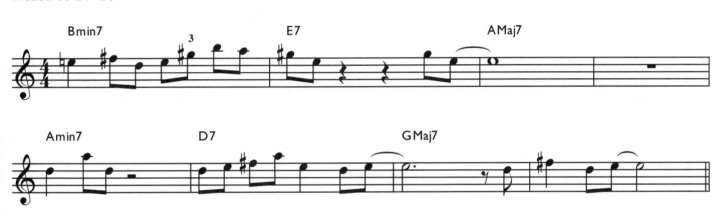

When the chords move even faster (as in the last four measures of the bridge), you can play the same thing in one key and then the next key. This will give continuity and symmetry even at a hectic pace.

Measures 29–32

ONLY WHAT YOU'RE NOT
(Standard Changes)

Roadmap

5 total choruses:
1 chorus of head, 1 chorus of saxophone solo, 2 choruses of piano solo, 1 chorus of head out.

Overview

"Only What You're Not" uses chord changes associated with the Jerome Kern standard "All the Things You Are" and also used on a range of modern jazz tunes from Charlie Parker's "Bird of Paradise" to Charles Mingus's tongue-in-cheek "All the Things You Could Be By Now If Sigmund Freud's Wife Was Your Mother." Most often played at a medium tempo, the song has a form that could be described as ABCA' with the B containing the same chords as the first A but a 4th away and the final A including an extra four-measure *tag*, or ending. The song also contains a good deal of modulation, going through no fewer than five major keys. As such, identifying the tonalities and knowing how to catch the modulations become vital. The result is an extremely stimulating group of chords that challenges our ability to maintain a melodic flow as the harmonic landscape shifts.

Listening Suggestions

"The Quintet" (Charlie Parker et. al): "All the Things You Are"

This music has been issued at different points under ensemble names and with different album names (*The Greatest Jazz Concert Ever* or *Jazz At Massey Hall*, referring to the Canadian venue). What hasn't changed is the potency of having Charlie Parker, Dizzy Gillespie, Bud Powell, Charles Mingus, and Max Roach sharing the stage and showing what made each of them so influential.

Art Blakey: "Prince Albert"

Trumpeter Kenny Dorham composed this bebop-infused melody over these chords and made a great recording of it with Max Roach. This live recording with the band of drummer Art Blakey, meanwhile, is the landmark version. Blakey holds it down alongside bassist Doug Watkins and pianist Horace Silver, while Dorham and saxophonist Hank Mobley each take strong solos.

Johnny Griffin: "All the Things You Are"

We hear Art Blakey again on this one, along with bassist Paul Chambers, pianist Wynton Kelly, and trumpeter Lee Morgan. What really makes this all-star recording sizzle, though, is the "tenor battle" in which Griffin engages in some good-spirited one-upsmanship with fellow tenor saxophonists Hank Mobley and John Coltrane. Collectively, they offer a clinic in navigating these chord changes.

Sonny Rollins and Coleman Hawkins: "All the Things You Are"

The tenor saxophone clinic continues here. Coleman Hawkins was the first widely influential tenor saxophonist, inspiring generations of younger players including Sonny Rollins, who also had a wide impact on subsequent generations. Rollins always drew upon earlier sounds and Hawkins was always more modern than one might expect from an "old-timer," so it stands to reason that their collaboration would come together well. Paul Bley also gets in a nice piano solo.

Improvising on "Only What You're Not"

This tune should be renamed "Will the True ii–V–I Please Step Forward?"

In this chord progression, the chords are tricky because it is not always obvious where they
are going. At first glance, it looks like the first chord is the ii and the next chord the V, but what
will stop astute chord analyzers in their tracks is that the second chord is minor. Going on to
the third and fourth chord is where it becomes clear that the second measure gives us the ii,
the third measure the V, and the fourth measure the anchor of our I chord. Once the correct
ii–V–I is identified, then soloing will make more sense. This same type of "deception" occurs in
measures 9–12 and 25-28, but the song is mostly made up of various ii–V–I's.

The first chord, Fmin7, is the vi chord, the relative minor of A♭ Major. Therefore, we can look at
those first four measures as being in A♭ Major. We'll use the A♭ Major scale, but to break up
the straight major tonality, let's try using the altered scale over the V chord.

Measures 1–4

In measures 5–8, we move from our A♭ Major tonality (with D♭Maj7 as the IV chord) to a C
Major tonality. This is a pretty drastic change because the only notes the two scales have
in common are G, F, and C. However, it is not hard to make a clear distinction between the
chords if we play the corresponding major scale over each chord (A♭ Major scale over D♭Maj7
and C Major scale over CMaj7). Below is a straight-up way to play over these changes.
Remember that G7 is just the V of CMaj7, so phrases using the C Major scale work well here.

Measures 5–7

Here's another approach over the same chords. Using the altered scale over the G7 will make a smoother transition because it adds more notes in common with the Ab Major scale; now, Ab, Bb, Db, and Eb will also be in common. This makes the tonalities a little closer, and then once you get to the CMaj7, the transition has a different sound.

Measures 5–7

When taking a vacation, a destination must be known before an airplane ticket is booked. The same is true in soloing. You must know all the tonal centers you will visit and then plan how to get there. In this case, looking ahead reveals that the tune doesn't stay in C Major for very long before heading toward Eb Major via a vi–ii–V–I–IV and then G Major via a V–I. The bridge stays in G Major for four measures and then goes to E Major. The end starts as the song began and then circles around to stay in the key of Ab Major, where it ends. Now that all the tonal centers are known, let's find an interesting way to get to more of them.

One way to do this is to anticipate an approaching chord by inserting the V chord that leads to it. For example, since we know the next chord in the progression is Cmin7 (the vi in Eb Major), let's take a path to get there from the CMaj7 by inserting a V chord a measure before our destination. In the example below, we are moving from CMaj7 to Cmin7, and we are using G7 as a way to get there, with the altered scale as our tool for soloing over that G7.

Measures 7–9

Below, we have the next two tonalities. Notice that over the V chords, we are using the altered scale.

Measures 9–15

HERE COMES BILL
(Modal)

Roadmap

5 total choruses:
1 chorus of head, 1 chorus of saxophone solo, 2 choruses of piano solo, 1 chorus of head out.

Overview

In place of traditional chord changes, "Here Comes Bill" uses a modal structure in which tonalities are used over longer stretches of time, in this case, eight measures of D Dorian for the A sections and eight measures of Eb Dorian for the bridge. In the vein of Miles Davis's "So What" and John Coltrane's subsequent "Impressions," these tonalities imply minor 7th chords but are typically approached in a more flexible, open-ended manner than that. With the reduced rate of harmonic motion, the results can be very straightforward and melodic (as in Miles's solo on the original "So What"), which is a big part of why modal songs like this are often played by people newer to improvising who are thus relieved of having to navigate chord changes as frequently. On the flip side, these open-ended structures can enable much more diverse, risk-taking approaches to chords and improvisation, a perspective typified by John Coltrane's work in the 1960s. The tempo for these harmonies can range from medium-slow to very brisk.

Listening Suggestions

Miles Davis: "So What"
The subtly swinging version from *Kind of Blue* was a watershed moment in modal jazz, featuring solos from Miles, John Coltrane, Cannonball Adderley, and Bill Evans. Miles continued playing the song for years, with multiple live versions from the mid-1960s featuring a much faster tempo and the innovative rhythm section work of Herbie Hancock, Ron Carter, and Tony Williams.

John Coltrane: "Impressions"
John Coltrane recorded "Impressions," an up-tempo working of these harmonies with his original melody, well over a dozen times in live performances between 1961 and 1965. His playing was consistently exploratory in his addressing of the harmonic possibilities within the open-ended structure, while he also exhibited a ferocious intensity, usually spurred by the hard-swinging and equally ferocious drumming of Elvin Jones.

George Benson: "So What"
Guitarist George Benson's ability to play authoritative straight-ahead jazz is matched by his command over the sounds of rock, pop, and R&B. On this track, he bridges the gap, spending some time soloing over an assertive swing groove and some time wailing over drummer Jack DeJohnette's funky backbeat. Bassist Ron Carter, who played the song so often with Miles Davis, gets a great solo turn as well.

McCoy Tyner: "Impressions"
Elvin Jones and Ron Carter are also present on this trio recording by pianist McCoy Tyner. Tyner is present on all of Coltrane's versions of "Impressions" but would often back off and even lay out altogether for minutes on end in order to give Coltrane more freedom. This inventive and rhythmically assertive performance shows once and for all that his willingness to give Coltrane the stage only camouflaged his own stunning command of these harmonies.

Improvising on "Here Comes Bill"

Pentatonic scale patterns are effective for soloing over modal progressions like this one. For this chord progression, D Minor Pentatonic can be used over the Dmin7 chord and E♭ Minor Pentatonic over the E♭min7 chord. Here are the scales starting on the roots of each chord.

Pentatonic scales are useful because they reveal the tonality of a given chord yet produce a very open and forgiving sound, with fewer potentially "wrong" notes and more "good" notes. Pentatonics also lend themselves to being played in rhythmic ways.

To get started playing patterns with a pentatonic scale, try a small three-note pattern. Take the first three notes of the pentatonic scale and play them straight up: D–F–G. Then, start on the next note in the scale and do the same pattern of three ascending notes: F–G–A. Keep going with this pattern through the scale. Once at the top of the line, start descending the pentatonic scale using the same pattern. Slurs are used here to signify each of the three-note phrases.

Now, try reversing the pattern. Instead of playing the three notes straight up, try playing them going down. The pattern now starts with G–F–D, then moves up to A–G–F, and so on.

Try mixing the two lines together. Try one when ascending and the other as the line descends.

Though any amount of notes can be used to create a pattern, four-note patterns are probably the most common. Below is the same idea as the three-note pattern from the previous page, but now with four notes. This example uses the combined approach, with notes going up when ascending the scale and notes going down when descending the scale. We'll play this over the E♭ Minor portion of the tune.

Practicing all the different permutations of a pattern will give a soloist many possibilities on a modal tune. Patterns don't always have to be straight up or down. Try using the pentatonic to create other types of patterns. Following is a familiar one, using one pattern for ascending (skipping notes in the pentatonic scale) and a different one for descending.

Here is one more example of using patterns. Can you figure out the pattern?

PHOTO COURTESY OF INSTITUTE OF JAZZ STUDIES, RUTGERS UNIVERSITY

*The impact of **Bill Evans** (1929–1980) on modern jazz piano is enormous. His rhythmic flexibility, interactivity with bass and drums, and rich voicings were all groundbreaking. He was a major contributor to the early development of modal jazz and his ballad playing influenced generations of musicians.*

Now that the patterns are flowing through your fingers, try adding some chords to round things out. The chords in a modal tune are just as important as the single-note lines. This is in part because, when modal jazz started, it was grounded in what we call *quartal* voicings. The term quartal refers to the use of 4ths, as opposed to the more typical *tertian* harmony (based on 3rds). The quartal sound is very open and lends itself to having other sounds superimposed on top of it. Quartal voicings are easiest described as any voicings that are primarily made up of 4ths. To create one, take the root of the chord and build up in 4ths. This works really well over minor chords (though it can be used on many different types of chords) and especially in a modal context. Below is an example of 4th voicings for left hand up the D Dorian mode.

The right hand can be added to the left hand to expand upon these chords. There are two main ways to approach the quartal voicings with both hands. First, there is the all-4ths approach, in which you simply add 4ths on top of each other. This creates a real open and sometimes dissonant sound. Be careful how and when you play these chords. This approach sounds great over a modal tune like this but will not always sound right in other tunes. Below are two-handed quartal voicings in D Minor.

Another commonly used quartal voicing features the same basic 4ths in the left hand with one added 4th in the right and then a 3rd on top of that. This is the sound associated with songs like "So What." Again, some of these can be really dissonant even in a modal tune, so you should be aware of what type of sound you are going for.

Following is a commonly used comping pattern for a modal tune. This features both the all-4th voicings and the "So What" voicings. Note that the right hand is only playing two notes instead of three—this is yet another option. Notice also the use of the root and 5th down low at the beginning of the phrase, a technique associated with McCoy Tyner.

Now, you have some tools at your fingertips for soloing on a modal tune. Try combining the left-hand ideas and the right-hand ideas. Below is a example of how to use all these ideas together over eight measures of Dmin7 and eight measures of E♭min7.

Boy from Penn Drive
(Latin)

Roadmap

5 total choruses:

1 chorus of head, 1 chorus of saxophone solo, 2 choruses of piano solo, 1 chorus of head out.

Overview

"Boy from Penn Drive," inspired by the great Brazilian composer Antônio Carlos Jobim and songs of his like "Garota de Ipanema" ("Girl from Ipanema"), represents the Brazilian style bossa nova. The term "Latin jazz" is so broad-based that it can refer to virtually any jazz-based music where even, or "straight," eighth notes are used in place of the swing eighth notes typical of most jazz. Authentically playing any of the substyles in the realm of Latin jazz requires a great deal of specific study, whether the samba rhythms of Brazil or the many rhythms under the umbrella of Afro-Cuban music. There are some global facets to playing with straight eighths; indeed in some jazz settings, the edict "play Latin" means basically that, with any effective hybrid of stylistic elements permissible. As a very common form of Latin jazz, it is important for a well-rounded jazz pianist to develop a basic awareness of bossa nova rhythms and comping patterns.

Listening Suggestions

Stan Getz and João Gilberto: "Girl from Ipanema (Garota de Ipanema)"
This track and the *Getz/Gilberto* album both enjoyed massive crossover success in 1965, solidifying and highlighting the infiltration of the bossa nova sound into the musical fabric of the United States. Cool-toned American tenor saxophonist Stan Getz, Brazilian singer/guitarist João Gilberto, and vocalist Astrud Gilberto were major figures in bossa nova, joined here by composer Antônio Carlos Jobim himself on piano.

Oscar Peterson: "Girl from Ipanema"
Oscar Peterson's trios were his calling card as a bandleader, and the incarnation with bassist Ray Brown and drummer Ed Thigpen is to some the epitome of what an elegant piano-bass-drums ensemble should be. This version of the Jobim classic does not use the standard bossa nova rhythm, instead adding a bit of swing feeling to find a bouncy Latin/swing middle ground for their infectious playing.

Sérgio Mendes: "Girl from Ipanema"
In the 1960s explosion of Brazilian jazz in the United States, pianist and bandleader Sérgio Mendes was a major figure, attaining significant crossover popularity for his jazz-inflected bossa novas, most often in a trio setting. On this performance, he finds a perfect addition in the cool-toned but harmonically sophisticated flugelhorn of modern jazz giant Art Farmer.

Eliane Elias: "Garota de Ipanema"
The traditions of Brazilian music are deep, but as with any art form, younger generations invariably look to balance the tradition with more modern and personal developments. Brazilian pianist and sometimes vocalist Eliane Elias epitomizes this, as she is equally conversant in both traditional and modern vocabularies, well-displayed on this rhythmically and harmonically forward-thinking arrangement and performance.

Improvising on "The Boy from Penn Drive"

"The Boy from Penn Drive" uses a bossa nova rhythm, which requires a slightly different approach than the previous etudes. The type of beat that will be discussed here is more of a jazz-based bossa than a traditional Brazilian bossa nova. This type of feel will fit into what is typically called "Latin jazz," which has a mix of elements from Latin-based rhythms and jazz rhythms.

Bossas should have a laid back and relaxed feel. Compared to a swinging tune, a bossa has a different type of rhythmic identity and flow. Straight-ahead jazz tunes are based on a swing rhythm, an uneven rhythmic eighth-note pattern. Also, beats 2 and 4 are emphasized. In contrast, bossa novas tend to use straight eighth notes, both in melodies and in the rhythm section. In addition, bossas also tend to emphasize beats 1 and 3 instead of the 2 and 4 of jazz. The strong beats on 1 and 3 (indeed, bossa beats could often be seen as being in the $\frac{2}{4}$ time signature) give an impression of swaying back and forth, creating that laid back feel.

Below is a standard comping pattern for a bossa. Notice the rhythm tends to repeat with predictability. As mentioned above, the strong beats for a bossa are 1 and 3, and the comping plays off those beats really well—notice there are many chords placed on the "and" of beats 2, 3, and 4. Also, notice that most of the voicings in this example are quartal voicings used over major, minor, and dominant chords.

Measures 1–8

Remember that there are many types of "Latin jazz." This is only one type and it is far-reaching to say this comping pattern will work for all Latin tunes. However, a general rule that does apply to all Latin jazz tunes is that the eighth notes are played straight and no longer swung. The same lines and ideas covered so far in this book can be used over Latin jazz tunes, just with a straight-8th feel.

An important part of this chord progression is the use of the *tritone substitution*. A *tritone* is the distance of three whole steps; this interval can also be referred to as an augmented 4th or diminished 5th. A tritone substitution is when a dominant chord is substituted for another dominant chord a tritone away. These substitutions work because the 3rds and 7ths of each chord are the same but in reverse. For example, in the A section, we have the G♭7 chord, in each case followed by FMaj7. The obvious choice to precede FMaj7 is a C7 (the V chord), but G♭7 is a tritone substitute for C7. This works because the C7 has E as its 3rd and B♭ as its 7th. The G♭7 chord has B♭ as its 3rd and E (the enharmonic equivalent of F♭) as its 7th. See how the 3rds and 7ths are the same except in reverse? Though the other notes in the chord are different, the common 3rd and 7th tones maintain the V–I resolution but with a slightly different feel.

Below are three turnarounds in F Major. The first uses the regular changes, the second uses tritone substitutions, and the last features the tritone substitution chords while maintaining the same bass notes as the first chord progression. This last option includes the ♯9 and ♯5 of the chords—real hip tones!

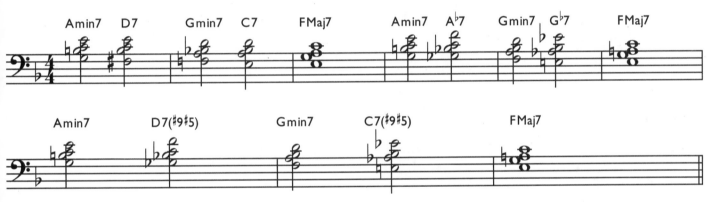

Not only is the tritone substitution a compositional tool, but it can be used while soloing as well. Let's try it on the turnaround of the bridge (the last four measures). Instead of Amin7–D7–Gmin7–C7, let's solo as if the changes were Amin7–A♭7–Gmin7–G♭7. The bass player can still imply the original chords but the soloist can add these changes and make the chords jump to life with alterations, just by thinking of different scales as the chords go by. Below is a simple example so you can easily recognize what is happening. Notice over the D7 that A♭ Mixolydian is being played, and over the C7, G♭ Mixolydian is being played.

Measures 21–24

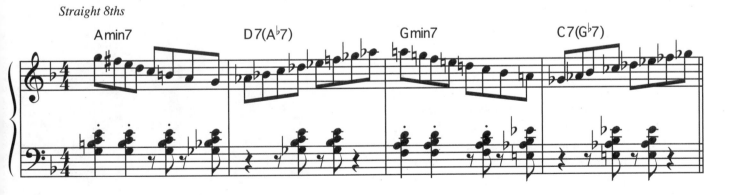

ABSTRACT FEELINGS
(Ballad)

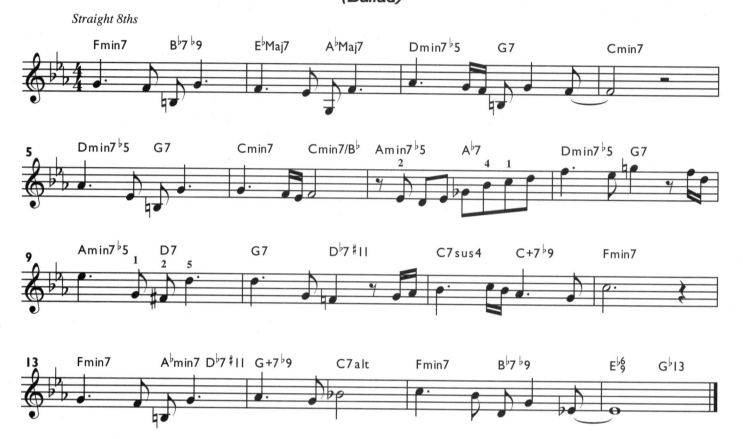

Roadmap

4 total choruses:
1 chorus of head, 1 chorus of saxophone solo, 1 chorus of piano solo, 1 chorus of head out.

*Thelonious Monk (1917–1982) was a unique figure
in jazz. His quirky, sometimes dissonant piano style
and unusual compositions were initially met with
some bewilderment, but his innovations soon became
fundamental to the sounds of modern jazz, and his
approach to ballads (both as a pianist and composer)
was highly important.*

PHOTO COURTESY OF INSTITUTE OF JAZZ STUDIES, RUTGERS UNIVERSITY

Overview

Learning how to authentically and effectively play ballads (a term that in this context refers to slow songs) is vitally important. There are several challenges specific to ballad playing. One is the lessening of rhythmic momentum. In modern jazz, ballads are typically played without swing eighth notes and thus without the propulsion that swing rhythms bring. Also, the slow tempo of a ballad means that whatever you play is more exposed. Some compensate for this by playing a lot of notes, but it is important to develop the ability to simply play lush, clean voicings and improvise in a manner that is lyrical and ideally somehow relevant to the song's melody. "Abstract Feelings" uses chords in the style of "I Fall In Love Too Easily," a Styne/Cahn song introduced in 1945 by Frank Sinatra but subsequently played and recorded by many jazz musicians. Indeed, most of the ballads in the jazz repertoire were pop songs and/or songs from musicals or films of the 1930s and 1940s.

Listening Suggestions

Chet Baker: "I Fall In Love Too Easily"
Chet Baker was an important interpreter of ballads, both as a vocalist and through his Miles Davis–inspired trumpet playing. In one of the best-loved versions of this song (from his 1956 *Chet Baker Sings* album) we are treated to both, and he imbues the song with tenderness throughout. Russ Freeman's flowing piano solo is also a highlight.

Miles Davis: "I Fall In Love Too Easily"
From "My Funny Valentine" to "It Never Entered My Mind" to "Lament," it seems as though every time Miles Davis played a ballad it became a definitive version of that song. His lyrical, Harmon-muted version of "I Fall In Love Too Easily," featuring elegant piano work from Victor Feldman and the warm, supple bass work of Ron Carter, is no exception.

Bill Evans: "I Fall In Love Too Easily"
Bill Evans' ballad playing is a wonderful context to hear some of his most influential traits, including his rich, lush chord voicings and his authoritative yet elastic sense of phrasing within a tempo. This short but substantial rendition from the *Moon Beams* album displays all of this, as well as the loose interactivity he established in his trio.

Shirley Horn: "I Fall In Love Too Easily"
Pianist and vocalist Shirley Horn was best known for her lovely ballad work, often deftly performing them at extremely slow tempos that in most musicians' hands would lose energy. Here, she gives her ballad treatment to this song in an all-star trio alongside bassist Ron Carter and drummer Al Foster, with Roy Hargrove joining in as a guest trumpet soloist.

Improvising on "Abstract Feelings"

Ballads are a great place to work on harmonizing melodies or melodic solo lines. There is nothing wrong with playing a melodic line in the right hand and chords in the left hand for a ballad. However, there will definitely be times when giving more "oomph" to the melodic line will be desired. Let's say that we want to create a solo piano introduction (a task definitely asked of any pianist at one time or another) to "Abstract Feelings." Following is an example of an introduction using the last four measures of "Abstract Feelings." Remember to play with a straight-eighth feel.

It is common to use material from the last four measures of a tune when creating an intro, as it produces a unified sense of feel and texture as well as a seamless transition. All the notes under the melodic line are harmonies that fit into the chord and fill in the space between the melody and the bass note. Be aware that the notes surrounding middle C (from about bass C up to treble C) represent prime real estate register-wise. This is where most chordal action will take place for a pianist, where voicings will have the desired impact and blend. The notes speak clearly here without being muddled, as with the low end of the piano, and this register has a strength that the high register lacks. When filling in chords under a melody, use this middle register as much as possible. The third and fourth measures of the intro use a four-note pattern that descends a few octaves. Pianistic approaches like this are more common on a ballad as they fill the space, and there is more time to fill due to the slower tempo.

As for which notes to use, this is partly up to an individual's taste and the larger musical context, or sometimes just plain physical habit. Remember, though, that after the melody and root, the 3rd and 7th are the most important chord tones to include in a voicing, as these tones determine whether the chord or scale is major, minor, or dominant.

Look at the intro's melodic line on the previous page. The melody note (G) of the first chord (Fmin7) is the 9th. In the left hand, we grab the shell voicing (see page 77) to make sure the root, 3rd, and 7th are represented. After the root, 3rd, and 7th are added to the left hand, there is not a lot of room between them and the 9th in the melody. There is only room for one more note, and the C (the 5th) is a nice evenly placed note. Placing notes evenly in a voicing like this can make it sound fuller. The rest of the first measure continues in the same way. The second measure starts with the same idea as the first (shell voicing in left hand and filled in with one extra note) but things change slightly at the altered C7. The shell voicing is used again, but the melody note is a little bit higher than in the previous chords, which means there is more room to add color notes. The ♯11 and ♯9 are added, and then on the fourth beat of the measure, those two notes lead to the 5 and ♭9. This type of inner-voice movement not only adds harmonic interest but also defines the time better than merely holding a note for two beats. The last addition is on the "and" of 4, where the tritone substitution is used (C7 instead of G♭7).

The next example shows one way of soloing over a ballad with a rhythm section. It is a single line that one might play over the first four measures.

Measures 1–4

Next, we have harmonized the line from above, with both hands working together to make the simple melodic line a bit fuller. We needn't always divide duties between right hand and left hand; thinking about both hands can give the solo a more coherent feel.

Measures 1–4

IT TAKES BIG FEET
(Modern)

Roadmap

10 total choruses:
2 choruses of head, 3 choruses of saxophone solo, 3 choruses of piano solo,
2 choruses of head out.

John Coltrane (1926–1967) *impacted the development of jazz more than once. His use of advanced diatonic chord progressions like the one in "Giant Steps" was mind-blowing in 1959, yet soon thereafter he became at least as influential through his quest to play modal jazz in a spiritually transcendent manner. From 1961–1965 he pursued this goal as the leader of one of the landmark ensembles in modern jazz, The John Coltrane Quartet with pianist McCoy Tyner, bassist Jimmy Garrison, and drummer Elvin Jones.*

PHOTO COURTESY OF INSTITUTE OF JAZZ STUDIES, RUTGERS UNIVERSITY

Overview

There are numerous jazz standards that can be used as up-tempo vehicles. In addition to rhythm changes and "Cherokee" changes addressed earlier in this book, "Just One of Those Things," "Lover," and "I'll Remember April" are just a few of the songs that jazz musicians use both to challenge themselves and to display their virtuosity with chord changes and bright tempos. In the late 1950s, saxophonist John Coltrane took this to an extreme with "Giant Steps," a song that is both very challenging and very logical. The whole song modulates among the major keys of B, G, and E♭ (all a major 3rd apart, thus outlining an augmented triad), consisting of V–I and ii–V–I progressions in those three keys. The challenge comes in the fast tempo and the frequency of the modulations (indeed, at no point do we have more than two measures to relax within a single tonality), all requiring a high degree of proficiency. "It Takes Big Feet" uses these now-standard chords.

Listening Suggestions

John Coltrane: "Giant Steps"

This recording, from the album by the same title, is the textbook for beginning to approach *Coltrane changes* as they are sometimes called. While on many other recordings we hear Coltrane's soulful and lyrical sides, the focus here is on his bar-raising fluency. Coltrane took the Coltrane-changes concept and applied it to numerous other compositions, including "Countdown," "Satellite," and "26-2."

Tete Montoliu: "Giant Steps"

The great and (at least in the United States) underappreciated Spanish pianist Tete Montoliu recorded multiple authoritative versions of "Giant Steps" in both trio and solo settings. Particularly impressive is the version on his trio set *Tete!* with Niels-Henning Ørsted Pedersen and Albert "Tootie" Heath. In all cases, we hear the required fluency combined with distinctive flow and flexibility.

Freddie Hubbard: "Dear John"

A significant associate of Coltrane's, trumpeter Freddie Hubbard wrote and performed this tribute song on his *Bolivia* album, using the "Giant Steps" progression. Also featured here are tenor saxophonist Ralph Moore and two others who recorded with Coltrane, pianist Cedar Walton (who actually played on the first-ever recording of "Giant Steps," which was initially unreleased) and drummer Billy Higgins.

Rahsaan Roland Kirk: "Giant Steps"

Multi-woodwind virtuoso Rahsaan Roland Kirk was fluent in a number of different settings, from soulful blues to bebop to avant-garde. The harmonic rigidity of "Giant Steps" might make it seem like an odd vehicle for combining these disparate musical worlds, but with a vocal choir and an ensemble featuring the powerful piano work of Hilton Ruiz, Kirk does precisely that.

Improvising on "It Takes Big Feet"

When a tune with Coltrane changes is called, musicians are often left shaking in their boots! It has the reputation of being a very challenging set of changes (which it is), but it is hardly insurmountable. There are ways to maneuver through the changes that make it fairly straightforward.

As with the changes we explored in "Carob Powder," it is a great idea to practice these ideas slowly. Speed comes with practice. Look at the chord progression. Remember, Coltrane changes modulate in major 3rds, and this is accomplished through the common V–I resolution. This tune uses a "family" of three keys, all a major 3rd apart: E♭ Major, G Major, and B Major.

The primary challenge with this tune is the pace at which these modulations occur. They move not only at a rapid tempo but also with a fast harmonic rhythm (usually two beats for each chord).

John Coltrane himself is probably the best example to follow, having devised these changes. The way he approached the tune was to stay close to the tonality of the chords. One way he did this was to play the root, 2nd, 3rd, and 5th of each chord (for example, B, C♯, D♯, and F♯ for BMaj7). Below is an example of this idea over the first three measures.

Measures 1–3

Another Coltrane approach that works well is to play the major triad of each chord as it goes by, as in the following example.

Measures 1–3

Now, practice the triads in different inversions. This makes the line sound less like an exercise and more like music.

Measures 1–3

Now, let's dig in and combine the root–2nd–3rd–5th approach and the triad approach.

Measures 5–7

To add a little color, try to incorporate some of the previously discussed diminished ideas (see pages 36–37) over the dominant 7th chords. However, in order to maintain a clear articulation of the changes, be sure to keep in place the approaches we just covered. Use an entire scale if the time allows, like when a chord lasts a full measure.

Below is an example over the first seven measures. Notice that it starts on the 5th of the chord (F♯ is the 5th of BMaj7). By starting on a note other than the root, we can produce a different sound and get to some new melodic and harmonic places.

Measures 1–7

Remember, this song is only in three keys. If you have proficiency in all three, then playing this tune should not be as difficult as one might think. The last part of the progression cycles through the ii–V–I in all three keys. Play an effective line in one, and you can transpose it to the other two, like below.

Measures 8–13

APPENDIX A: SCALES

The first thing we'll pull out of our toolbox is *scales*. Most scales in Western music are made up of a specific pattern of *half steps* and *whole steps*. A half step is the shortest distance between two notes. Two half steps make a whole step.

A Note About Fingering Scales

Before you actually begin to play the major scales on page 71, it's worth taking a moment to develop some strategies for fingering. Most effective scale fingerings are based on a few basic principles that can be applied to virtually any scale.

- Most traditional scale fingerings are based on the principle of efficiency—that is, minimizing unnecessary motion such as excessive finger crossing. If you cross over (or under) every two notes, you're probably not using the most effective fingering; if you find yourself running out of fingers, you're probably not crossing often enough.

- Avoid using your thumb on black keys. Finger crossing almost always involves the thumb, and if the thumb avoids black keys, the chances of getting tangled are greatly lessened. Most standard fingerings, especially for scales with many black keys, ensure that the thumb always lands on a white key.

- When playing scales, use your 5th finger only on the lowest note (left hand) or highest note (right hand) of the scale. Crossing to or from the 5th finger will land you in an awkward position.

- Look ahead as you play and watch for signposts that suggest fingering strategies. For example, be attentive to how many notes are left in the passage, or how many black keys come before the next white key. Observations like these will help you determine what you need to do to avoid running out of fingers or crossing too often.

- Similar scales often have similar fingerings. Unless it involves a violation of the previous guidelines, you can often apply the fingering for one scale to a different scale that begins on the same note. If you know the fingering for the C Major scale, for example, you can use it for most other seven-note scales that begin on C.

Major Scales

The *major scale*, shown below in the key of C, has the following pattern of half and whole steps. Notice the numbers underneath; these are *degrees*, which show each note's position within the scale.

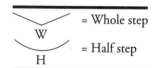

Major Scale

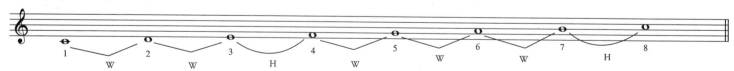

Below are all 12 major scales, including their traditional fingerings. Right-hand fingerings are shown above the staff; left-hand fingerings are shown below the staff. Notice that in some instances, two different finger numbers are shown for the same note. Use the number closer to the staff for endings or beginnings of scales, and the other number for scales that continue beyond one octave.

R.H. = Right Hand
L.H. = Left Hand

C Major (no accidentals)   G Major (one sharp)

D Major (two sharps)   A Major (three sharps)

E Major (four sharps)   B Major (five sharps)

G♭ Major (six flats)   D♭ Major (five flats)

A♭ Major (four flats)   E♭ Major (three flats)

B♭ Major (two flats)   F Major (one flat)

Other scales and keys can be used when *enharmonic equivalents* are employed. An enharmonic equivalent is a note that has a different name than another note but sounds the same. For example, the enharmonic equivalent of G♭ is F♯. So, there can be a key of F♯, which has six sharps (F♯, C♯, G♯, D♯, A♯, E♯). Also, the key of B could be enharmonically respelled as C♭ (seven flats: B♭, E♭, A♭, D♭, G♭, C♭, F♭), and the key of D♭ could be enharmonically respelled as C♯ (seven sharps: F♯, C♯, G♯, D♯, A♯, E♯, B♯).

Minor Scales

Minor scale is actually a general reference to several different scale forms. The most basic form of the minor scale is the *natural minor*, which you can think of as a major scale with a lowered 3rd (♭3), lowered 6th (♭6), and lowered 7th (♭7).

Natural Minor Scale

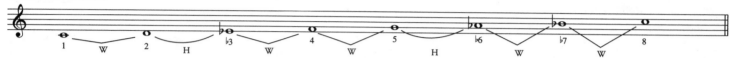

You can think of the *harmonic minor* scale as a major scale with ♭3 and ♭6. As the name implies, harmonic minor has traditionally been the form of the minor scale from which harmonies are most often derived, though it's also used in melodic contexts.

Harmonic Minor Scale

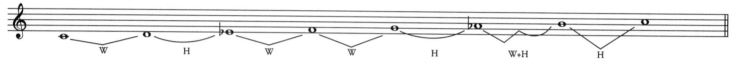

The *melodic minor* scale uses one form when ascending and another when descending. In its ascending form, you can think of melodic minor as a major scale with a ♭3. In its descending form, melodic minor is the same as natural minor (♭3, ♭6, and ♭7). When only the ascending form is used, the scale is often called the *jazz melodic minor* scale.

Melodic Minor Scale

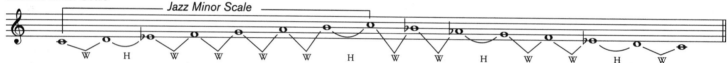

Pentatonic Scales

A *pentatonic scale* is any scale made up of five different notes. Two forms of pentatonic are especially common in jazz. In relation to the major, the *major pentatonic scale* is made up of scale degrees 1, 2, 3, 5, and 6. You can also think of this scale as a major scale with scale degrees 4 and 7 omitted.

The *minor pentatonic scale* is made up of scale degrees 1, ♭3, 4, 5, and ♭7. It can also be thought of as a natural minor scale with scale degrees 2 and 6 omitted.

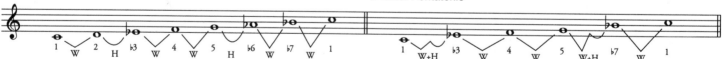

Blues Scale

In relation to the major scale, the blues scale is made up of scale degrees 1, ♭3, 4, ♭5, 5, and ♭7. You can also think of the blues scale as a minor pentatonic scale with the addition of ♭5.

C Blues

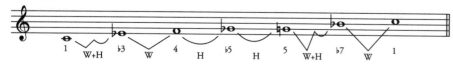

MODES OF THE MAJOR SCALE

The Greek-named modes of a major scale use the pitches of that scale, but with different starting notes. For example, the C Major scale has seven modes. Notice that the Ionian mode is simply the major scale, and the Aeolian mode is the natural minor scale. Each mode has a chord associated with it, shown in parentheses.

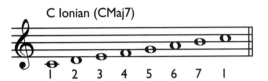

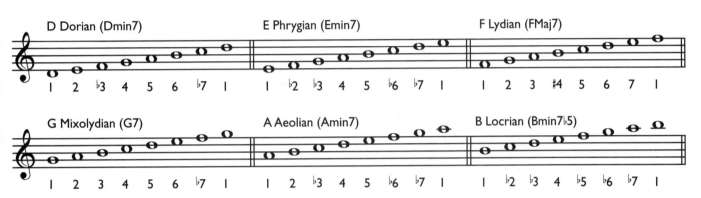

Each major scale has the same seven modes, using the same formula. The numbers under the modes above show how each mode's notes relate to the major scale with the same starting note. So, in figuring the scale degrees for D Dorian, we are not applying the degrees from the original C Major Scale (D=2, E=3, F=4, etc.); rather, we are deriving the scale degrees from the mode's parallel major scale (in this case, D Major). Learn the modes as scales unto themselves, each with its own pattern of intervals; to use a mode when improvising, you don't want to go through the step of first finding the corresponding major "parent" scale and then deriving the mode. So, to practice the Mixolydian mode, for example, look at the numbers underneath and notice that you have a major scale, but with a flatted 7th. Apply that formula in each key, with the corresponding chord in the left hand, and you have a great Mixolydian practice routine.

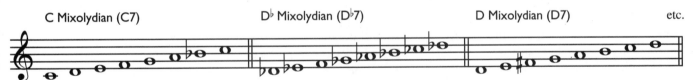

The Mixolydian mode can be played over a dominant 7th chord built from the same note. There are two other modes that are also particularly useful in modern jazz. The Dorian mode is extremely useful on minor chords—the natural 6th degree in Dorian (as opposed to the ♭6th in natural minor) makes Dorian's nice, open sound equally applicable to minor 7th and minor 6th chords. The Lydian mode, meanwhile, has a ♯4, which translated into an extension would be ♯11. As a result, the mode works perfectly with major chords, containing all of the colors typically associated with that chord type.

Modes of Melodic Minor as Autonomous Scales

As with the modes of the major scale, the modes of melodic minor can and should be learned as scales unto themselves. Each mode implies not only a chord, but specific color tones as well. For example, three modes imply dominant 7th chords, but each with different colors.

Mode	Numeric Formula	Chord Implied	Chord Colors Implied
Melodic Minor	1, 2, ♭3, 4, 5, 6, 7, 1	min/Maj7 (or min6)	9, 11, 13(6)
Dorian ♭2	1, ♭2, ♭3, 4, 5, 6, ♭7, 1	min7 (or min6)	♭9, 11
Lydian Augmented	1, 2, 3, ♯4, ♯5, 6, 7, 1	Maj7♯5	9, ♯11, 13
Lydian ♭7	1, 2, 3, ♯4, 5, 6, ♭7, 1	Dominant 7	9, ♯11, 13
Mixolydian ♭6	1, 2, 3, 4, 5, ♭6, ♭7, 1	Dominant 7	9, 11(4), ♭13(♯5)
Locrian ♯2	1, 2, ♭3, 4, ♭5, ♭6, ♭7, 1	min7♭5	9, 11
Altered	1, 2, ♭3, 3, ♭5, ♭6, ♭7, 1	Dominant 7	♭9, ♯9, ♭5, ♯5

The Bebop Scale

The *bebop scale* is a helpful change-making tool with a bebop sound. Actually, there are two bebop scales, one for dominant chords, one for minor 7th chords. Check them both out in C.

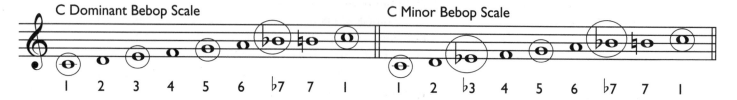

The dominant bebop scale resembles the Mixolydian mode and the minor bebop scale resembles the Dorian mode. In both cases, the difference is an added chromatic passing tone between the ♭7 and the tonic. This gives us eight-note scales, and in each case, every other note is a chord tone. Therefore, if you play eighth notes and you start with any chord tone on a downbeat, you can play the scale indefinitely (or at least until the chord changes) and hit a chord tone on every downbeat.

More Scales: Symmetrical Scales

A *symmetrical scale* is any scale based on the repetition of a single interval or pattern of intervals. These scales can sound great and their symmetry and regularity simplifies the learning process, since learning any of these scales depends only on remembering the pattern upon which the scale is based. One interesting feature of symmetrical scales is that, unlike major or minor scales, a symmetrical scale built on one note will always have a corresponding scale on another note that will yield the same exact pitches; we'll look at this feature below.

Diminished Scales

The commonly used symmetrical scales below are most often referred to as *diminished scales*. There are two different types of diminished scales, each made up of alternating half steps and whole steps.

The *half-whole diminished scale* is based on the pattern of a half step followed by a whole step. This scale is typically used with dominant 7th chords, and implies a ♭9, ♯9, ♯11, and 13.

C Half-Whole Diminished Scale

The *whole-half diminished scale* is typically used with diminished 7th chords. It is based on a pattern of a whole step followed by a half step.

C Whole-Half Diminished Scale

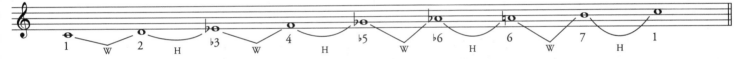

Each of these scales can be seen as a mode of the other. For example, if you begin on the second degree of a whole-half diminished scale, you end up with a half-whole scale. As mentioned above, the symmetry of these scales means that there are only really three different diminished scales of either type. For example, if you build a diminished scale on the 3rd degree of either of the examples we've looked at, the pitches will be exactly the same as those in the original scale. Another way to look at it is that the C, E♭, G♭, and A whole-half diminished scales all use the same eight pitches, as do the D, F, A♭, and B half-whole diminished scales, so that all eight of these scales are modes of one another.

Whole-Tone Scale

The *whole-tone scale* is a six-note scale made up entirely of whole steps. This scale is quite useful with dominant 7th chords (note its prevalence in the solos of Thelonious Monk), and implies a 9, ♭5, and ♯5. Because of their symmetrical nature, there are only two different whole-tone scales, one beginning on C, the other on C♯.

C Whole-Tone Scale   C♯ Whole-Tone Scale

It can also be used on tonic minor chords, but only if you use the scale that starts a half step away from the root!

B Whole-Tone Scale

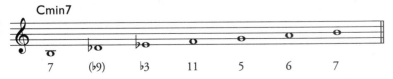

APPENDIX B: CHORDS AND HARMONIC DEVICES

Basic Chord Voicings

A *voicing* is the specific way a chord is played ("voicing" can also be used as a verb to refer to the process of coming up with a specific way to play a chord). In jazz, this is an essential tool. Since jazz chords tend to be rich-sounding 7th chords, a lot of attention is devoted to arranging the notes and deciding which notes are or aren't necessary to play, or which notes can be added to the chord for a richer sound. Add the issue of voice leading, and we have a lot to explore.

Rootless Voicing

One of the first steps in developing fluency with voicings is to become comfortable with the *rootless voicings*. The idea here is that if you are playing with a bassist (or practicing in preparation for playing with a bassist), he or she will likely be playing the root of each chord. As such, you can leave the roots out of your chords and simply play the remaining notes, generally the 3rd, 5th, and 7th. Your job then is to find smooth voice leading from each voicing to the next. Here are three ways of getting through a ii–V–I progression in the key of G using this voicing style. The left hand plays the root for extra reinforcement.

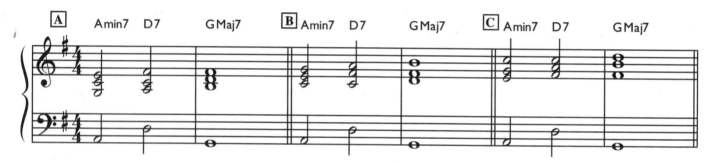

One thing to keep in mind is that when playing left-hand chords, issues of range become more important. The D below middle C is generally considered to be a cutoff point. That is, playing chords there or above is cool. If you play anything besides the root of the chord below that D, you are running the risk of making the chord sound muddy.

"Cutoff Point"

Now play the example above, but with the left hand playing the chords with no roots. Rootless voicings are an essential jazz tool because they avoid clashing or redundancy with the bass and leave the right hand free to solo and/or play melodies. The example below uses a progression in the style of the opening to Duke Ellington's "Satin Doll," with left-hand rootless voicings.

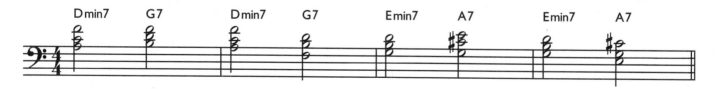

Shell Voicings

Next, we will explore *shell voicings*, a "skeletal" type of voicing that forms the basis for many other chord techniques. In a shell voicing, you omit the 5th, playing only the 3rd and 7th (plus the root down below, unless it is a rootless voicing). The basis for shell voicings is the realization that most 7th chords used in jazz sound just fine without the 5th. Play through the first three chords below and notice that the 5th of each chord is identical. Thus, if you leave out the 5th, you still have all the information you need to identify the chords.

For every 7th chord, there are two possible shell voicings, one with the 3rd on the bottom and one with the 7th on the bottom. Voice leading with shells tends to be extremely smooth. This is demonstrated below with two sets of shell voicings for a ii–V–I in the key of C Major. You can also play them with your right hand with left-hand roots underneath.

Bebop-Style Voicings

Bebop-style voicings, popularized by the great pianist Bud Powell, offer an even more skeletal chord option. For these left-hand voicings, you play the root on the bottom and either a 3rd or a 7th (but not both) on top. The top notes in the voicings should use smooth voice leading and stay above the "cutoff point" demonstrated on the previous page, even as the roots jump around and go low at times. Here are two sets of voicings in this style, each spelling out a ii–V–I in the key of F Major.

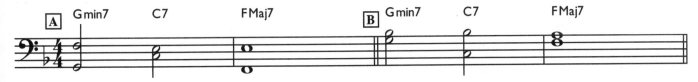

The bebop era, which began in the 1940s, brought new levels of virtuosity to soloing. These voicings stay low enough to give the right hand more room, giving enough information to put the right-hand lines in context as they more fully flesh out the sound of the chords.

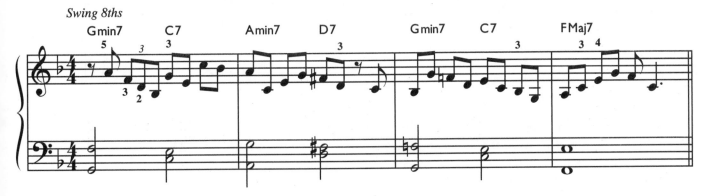

Four-Note Voicings

Thanks to the influential work of pianists like Bill Evans and Wynton Kelly, the rootless voicings we will explore on this page have become standard fare for modern jazz players. These voicings are particularly useful in the left hand, in tandem with right-hand solos or melodies. They are sometimes referred to as *A and B voicings* or *Bill Evans voicings*, though they are so common that there is generally no need to even call them by a name.

The basic formula is to take a shell and add the 5th and the 9th. One of these notes will go in between the notes in the shell, while the other note goes above. As such, the formula from the bottom up is either 3, 5, 7, 9 or 7, 9, 3, 5. Observe this on a CMaj7 chord.

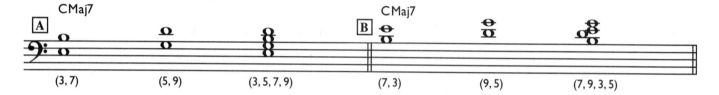

If you follow this formula and you are conscious of the voice leading in the shells, the voice leading overall will generally be very smooth. This is true even if you replace the 5th on the major and/or dominant chords with a 13th or use altered notes on the dominants.

Two-Handed Voicings

This next voicing style is a subtle and very cool variation on the Bill Evans–style voicings above. The idea here is to spread out the notes a little for a fuller sound and to take advantage of having both hands available at times when somebody else is playing the melody or solo, and you are only responsible for the chords.

You can form these voicings using the *drop 2 approach*, which simply means that you take the second note from the top and drop it down an octave. Notice the transformation.

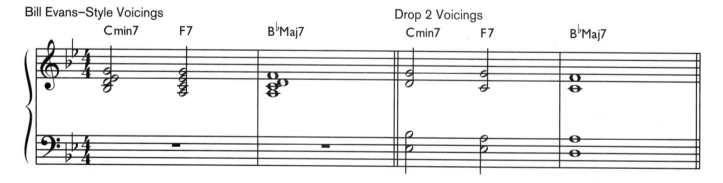

What you will see is that the division of labor between the hands becomes very clear-cut. The left hand plays the shell (3 and 7), while the right hand plays the other two more decorative notes (5 and 9 or variations thereof) directly above. If you are comfortable with your shells, then it can be very useful to think of it this way—the whole process becomes straightforward and the voice leading is as smooth as with the one-handed variation.

Diatonic Harmony

Diatonic Harmony in Major Keys

Diatonic means "of the scale," so the most basic definition of *diatonic harmony* is the chords built from a particular scale. While diatonic harmony itself isn't an improvisational tool, any jazz improviser must be able to identify the keys to which the chords in a tune relate, and how those chords function in those keys. One way to build these chords is to stack 3rds on each degree of the scale. In the case of 6th chords, you simply add a 6th above the root. (Note that in improvisational situations, 6th chords are often used in place of Maj7 chords.) Below are the diatonic 7th chords in the key of C. Note the use of Roman numerals under the music. They are discussed below.

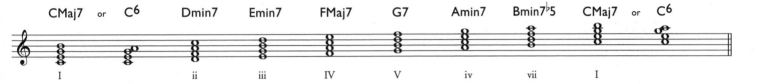

We use Roman numerals to signify the scale degree a chord is built on, since they're not specific to a particular key. We use uppercase Roman numerals for chords with a major 3rd (major, augmented, major 6, major 7, and dominant 7) and lowercase for those with a minor 3rd (minor, diminished, minor 7, minor 6, minor 7 flat five, and diminished 7). Here's a quick review of the Roman numerals you'll need and their Arabic equivalents:

ROMAN NUMERAL	ARABIC EQUIVALENT
I or i	1
II or ii	2
III or iii	3
IV or iv	4
V or v	5
VI or vi	6
VII or vii	7

Notation using Roman numerals is useful because the kind of chord built on each degree is the same in every key. Here are the diatonic 7th chords that you'll find in every major key:

DEGREE	QUALITY
I	Maj7/6
ii	min7
iii	min7
IV	Maj7
V	Dom7
vi	min7
vii	min7♭5

As a tool for memorizing the diatonic chords in every key, you can make yourself a chart like this:

KEY	I	ii	iii	IV	V	vi	vii
C	CMaj7	Dmin7	Emin7	FMaj7	G7	Amin7	Bmin7♭5
G	GMaj7	Amin7	Bmin7	CMaj7	D7	Emin7	F#min7♭5
Continue through all the keys in the cycle of 5ths.							

Diatonic Harmony in Minor Keys

The most obvious way to find the diatonic 7th chords in a minor key is to look at the relative major key, borrow the chords, and shift the Roman numerals. Here are the diatonic 7th chords for A Minor, the relative minor of C Major:

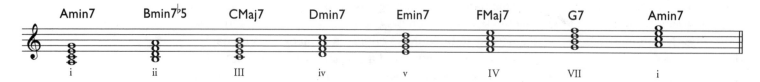

It doesn't end there, however. What you see above is based on the natural minor scale. But as we know, the natural minor is only one of three types of minor scales (see page 72). The primary use of the harmonic minor scale is just as the name implies—it's a scale from which harmonies are derived. This is because it provides a dominant 7 chord on V. Here are the diatonic 7th chords of an A Harmonic Minor scale:

As we can see, the i chord in harmonic minor is a minor chord with a major 7th (min/Maj7 or minn7) and the III chord is a major 7 chord with a raised 5th (Maj7#5). These are both unusual chords that sound most appropriate in a very modern setting.

In real musical situations, chords from both the natural and harmonic minor scales are used side by side—most often, i and III from natural minor, V and vii from harmonic minor, and the ii, iv, and VI common to both. Sometimes, a min6 chord is used in place of the min7 i chord.

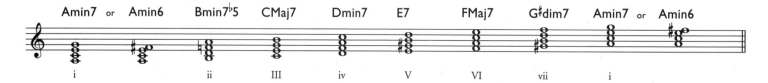

ii–V–I

In both major and minor keys, jazz harmony makes particularly frequent use of the progression ii–V–I (or, in minor, ii⌀–V–i). The V creates tension and gravity, pulling us "home" to I, and the ii extends and therefore intensifies that journey. Fluency in ii–V–I in all keys is one of the most important tools in a jazz musician's arsenal for playing and for analyzing chord progressions.

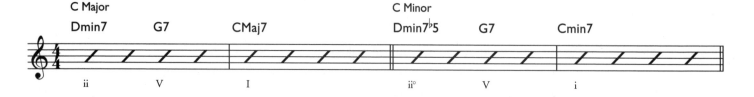